W9-ATT-283

Juicing

Publications International, Ltd.

Copyright © 2013 Publications International, Ltd.
All rights reserved. This publication may not be reproduced or quoted in whole or in part by any means whatsoever without written permission from:

Louis Weber, CEO
Publications International, Ltd.
7373 North Cicero Avenue
Lincolnwood, IL 60712

Permission is never granted for commercial purposes.

Photography on pages 25, 27, 29, 31, 33, 35, 37, 39, 41, 43, 45, 47, 49, 51, 53, 55, 59, 61, 63, 65, 67, 69, 71, 73, 75, 77, 79, 81, 83, 87, 89, 91, 93, 95, 97, 99, 101, 103, 105, 107, 109, 111, 115, 117, 119, 121, 123, 125, 129, 131, 133, 135, 137, 139, 141, 143, 145, 147, 149, 151, 153, 155, 157, 161, 163, 165, 169, 171, 173, 175, 177, 179, 181, 183 and 185 by PIL Photo Studio North.

Photography on front cover by Shutterstock.
Interior Art: Dreamstime, Fotofolio, iStockphoto, Photos to Go, PIL Collection, Shutterstock and Thinkstock.

Pictured on the back cover *(top to bottom):* Kiwi Twist *(page 114)*, Orchard Crush *(page 26)* and Cold and Flu Ninja Juice *(page 88)*.

ISBN-13: 978-1-4508-6799-3
ISBN-10: 1-4508-6799-5

Library of Congress Control Number: 2013935012

Manufactured in China.

8 7 6 5 4 3 2 1

Note: This publication is only intended to provide general information. The information is specifically not intended to be a substitute for medical diagnosis or treatment by your physician or other health care professional. You should always consult your own physician or other health care professionals about any medical questions, diagnosis, or treatment.

The information obtained by you from this book should not be relied upon for any personal, nutritional, or medical decision. You should consult an appropriate professional for specific advice tailored to your specific situation. PIL makes no representations or warranties, express or implied, with respect to your use of this information.

In no event shall PIL, its affiliates or advertisers be liable for any direct, indirect, punitive, incidental, special, or consequential damages, or any damages whatsoever including, without limitation, damages for personal injury, death, damage to property, or loss of profits, arising out of or in any way connected with the use of any of the above-referenced information or otherwise arising out of the use of this book.

Publications International, Ltd.

Table of Contents

Juicing 101 4
Apples 24
Apricots 30
Asparagus 32
Basil 34
Beets 36
Bell Peppers 40
Blackberries 42
Blueberries 44
Bok Choy 46
Broccoli 48
Brussels Sprouts 50
Butternut Squash 52
Cabbage 54
Cantaloupe 57
Carrots 60
Cauliflower 64
Celery 66
Cherries 70
Chile Peppers 72
Cilantro 74
Coconut Water 76
Cranberries 78
Cucumbers 80
Currants 85
Fennel 86
Garlic 88
Ginger 90
Grapefruit 94
Grapes 98
Green Beans 100
Greens 102
Honey 104

Honeydew 106
Jicama 108
Kale 110
Kiwi 113
Lemons 116
Limes 120
Mangoes 124
Mint 127
Onions 130
Oranges 132
Papaya 136
Parsley 138
Parsnips 140
Peaches 142
Pears 144
Pineapple 148
Plums 152
Pomegranates 154
Radishes 156
Raspberries 159
Spinach 162
Sprouts 164
Strawberries 167
Sweet Potatoes 170
Swiss Chard 172
Tangerines 174
Tomatoes 176
Turnips 180
Watercress 182
Watermelon 184
Zucchini 186
Index 187

Raise a Glass to Your Health

If your idea of juice is limited to that little glass of OJ next to your breakfast plate, you're in for a delicious, nutritious surprise. You can enjoy juices from a cornucopia of colorful, flavorful fruits and vegetables using an electric juicer and the simple recipes and tips in this book. As you'll quickly discover, juicing is an easy and convenient way to fit more fresh produce into your daily diet. And that's a proven path to better health and a lower risk of disease.

Why Start Juicing?

We've all heard the news—from doctors, nutritionists, the media and even the U.S. government: We need to eat more fruits and vegetables. These gifts from the garden (and orchard) are naturally rich sources of many of the vitamins and minerals that are essential to life. But more than that, research has shown time and again that getting plenty of fruits and vegetables can help us function at our best and protect us from a host of health problems, including heart disease and certain cancers. Scientists suspect these benefits come from the unique combinations of nutrients—including vitamins, minerals and special plant chemicals called phytonutrients—that are naturally present in produce. Studies using supplements of the most promising individual nutrients just don't produce the same health rewards.

With so much to gain, it just makes good sense to give fruits and vegetables a major place in our daily meals. Indeed, many experts say we should aim to fill half of our plate with fruits and vegetables at every meal. And the greater the variety of produce we choose, the more likely we are to cover our nutritional bases and gain the widest protection against everyday ills and chronic diseases.

Sadly, most of us don't come close to getting the minimum 2 cups of fruits and 2½ cups of vegetables a day that are recommended in the government's latest Dietary Guidelines for Americans. If you're one of those people—if you struggle to get the amount or variety of produce that your body deserves on a daily basis—juicing can help you bridge the gap. Juicing is also a great way to give yourself some additional, natural "health insurance."

You might think all juices are good for you, but seemingly healthy options can sometimes be deceiving. That fruity juice drink, for example, may actually contain less than 10 percent actual juice from fruit—and not necessarily from the fruit touted on the label. The rest of the carton or bottle may be filled with little more than artificial flavoring, artificial coloring and sugar water. But when you have a juicer, you can quickly turn fresh fruits and vegetables into delicious, invigorating juices that retain a high percentage of the original produce's vitamins, minerals and phytonutrients. Plus, you can control what goes into the machine, so you can be sure the resulting juices aren't loaded with sugar, salt or other additives that you don't need or want.

Using a juicer also makes exploring new produce options very simple. Preparing most fruits and vegetables for juicing often involves little more than washing the produce and feeding it into your juicer. The recipes in this book show you how to use more than 50 kinds of produce to create some truly delicious juices. In the process of trying those recipes, you're sure to come across plenty of fruits and vegetables that you'll want to start adding to your plate as well as your juicer.

But what if you (or other members of your household) simply aren't that into fruits or, more commonly, vegetables? What if your fork rarely strays beyond vegetable standbys like corn, potatoes and iceberg lettuce—unless, of course, there's plenty of fatty cheese, butter, gravy or dressing on hand? What if the closest you typically come to a serving of fruit is a slice of watermelon in the summer, a smear of strawberry jelly on your toast or the bananas in your banana split?

Truthfully, juicing alone can't make up for an overall poor diet. Even if you create and enjoy juice from a variety of produce each day, you still need to make the effort

Just To Be Safe

If you have a chronic medical condition, have been prescribed a special diet or take medication regularly, you should talk to your doctor or other health care provider about your interest in juicing before you begin. While adding fresh juices to the diet is typically a safe and healthful practice for most people, your health care provider may have some specific advice or warnings for you. Individuals taking certain medications, for example, need to avoid consuming grapefruit juice because of a potential negative interaction. And those with diabetes may need help determining how juices will affect their blood sugar and/or insulin needs. So always keep your health care team informed.

to include as many whole fruits and vegetables into your daily menu as possible. Your health depends on it. Because even though most of the vitamins, minerals and phytonutrients from the whole produce make it into the freshly made juice, the fiber does not. And that fiber contributes to many of the healing effects associated with fruits and vegetables.

Still, juicing can be a valuable part of a healthy diet. It can help fill the gaps when your produce intake falls short and provide your body with extra doses of disease-fighting nutrients. You can use it as an easy way to sample a wide variety of fruits and vegetables. You may even find yourself drinking juices made with vegetables you're not fond of because they've been combined with other fruits or vegetables that you do like. And that's far healthier than using a thick coating of cheese or gravy to make a food more appealing.

Types of Juicers

Some of juicing's growing popularity is due to advances in juicing technology. While an old-fashioned citrus juicer can turn out a fine glass of orange or grapefruit juice, the latest high-powered electric juice extractors can quickly juice a gamut of fruits and vegetables—from apples and asparagus to watermelon and zucchini. They also tend to be fairly easy to operate and are available in a range of models to fit most budgets.

more juice from the pulp than do centrifugal juicers. But masticating juicers also tend to be heavier, bulkier and more expensive than centrifugal juicers.

In a centrifugal juicer, a sharp, rotating metal blade or shredding disk grates the fruits and vegetables, and as the pieces spin around in a mesh basket, centrifugal force separates the juice from the pulp. Some centrifugal juicers have an automatic pulp ejector that sends the pulp into a side container once the juice has been extracted from it; this feature helps to make cleanup quicker and easier. Another useful feature available on some centrifugal juicers is an extra-wide mouth that allows you to feed larger pieces of fruits or vegetables (sometimes even whole fruits) into the machine, thus reducing or eliminating time spent cutting up produce for the juicer.

The electric juice extractors that can handle a wide range of produce come in two main types: masticating (also known as cold press because they do not produce heat as they extract the juice) and centrifugal. A masticating juicer works by smashing fruits and vegetables, much as our teeth crush food, and then using intense pressure to squeeze out the juice. Masticating juicers are quieter and tend to extract

Compared to masticating juicers, centrifugal juicers tend to be somewhat faster, easier to operate and clean, more affordable and more widely available. They are also more popular. For these reasons, the information and recipes in this book were developed with the centrifugal type of juicer in mind.

Help!

If you misplace your juicer's manual or have additional questions regarding proper care or operation, check the manufacturer's website. You can often view and download a copy of the manual for free and may even be able to access technical help. You may also find additional troubleshooting information and advice from the manufacturer.

Using and Caring for Your Juicer

Using your juicer correctly and taking proper care of it will help to extend its life, prevent problems with the machine and ensure that you get the greatest amount and quality of juice from it. The following tips can make doing so easier.

● Before you use your juicer for the first time, be sure to thoroughly read the manual supplied by the manufacturer. This can't be emphasized enough. While the information in this book generally applies to centrifugal juicers, it's important for you to read and follow the specific instructions, warnings and recommendations in the manual provided by the manufacturer of your machine. Not doing so may result in injury to you, damage to the machine, less than optimal juicing results and/or voiding of any warranties on the juicer. Once you begin using your machine, keep the manual handy for quick reference. It often contains helpful tips on preparing different types of produce for the best results.

● Be sure to use your juicer on a solid surface that's clean, dry and level. Position it well away from the edge of the surface so that vibration or an accidental nudge does not send it tumbling to the floor.

● Use extreme caution in handling any blades or other sharp parts when assembling, disassembling or cleaning your juicer.

● If your juicer comes with a tool for pushing fruits and vegetables into the machine, use it whenever you add produce to your machine; do not use your fingers or a kitchen tool instead. Press firmly but slowly on the pusher to maximize the amount of juice extracted.

● Before juicing hard fruits or vegetables, check the manual to determine if the machine needs to be stopped at intervals to prevent excess strain on the motor.

● To help keep pulp from clogging machine parts, alternate soft and hard produce whenever possible.

● Do not pour liquid or extremely soft ingredients—such as water, juice, yogurt or applesauce—into the juicer unless the manual states that you may do so.

● Be diligent about thoroughly cleaning your juicer after each use. Carefully following the manufacturer's cleaning instructions will not only help to keep the juicer in good working order, it can help protect you from food poisoning caused by the growth of harmful bacteria on the machine's parts.

● Be sure the unit is turned off and unplugged before disassembling and/or cleaning the machine.

● Never submerge the base unit (containing the motor) in water. Follow the instructions in the manual, which typically call for wiping down the unit with a damp soft cloth or nonabrasive sponge.

● Remove and wash the detachable parts of the juicer immediately after use, or at least rinse or soak them to help keep pulp from drying on the surfaces.

● Parts of the juicer that are dishwasher safe (check the manual) should typically be placed on the top shelf only.

● To make cleanup quicker and easier, use a disposable plastic produce bag to line your juicer's pulp-collection container (unless the manual directs otherwise). Once you've finished juicing, simply lift the bag out of the pulp container and discard the pulp, set it aside for use in other recipes, or add it to your garden or compost pile.

● If brightly colored fruits or vegetables (such as berries or beets) have left stains on washable plastic parts of your machine, try soaking the parts in water to which you've added a small amount of lemon juice.

Tips for Better Juicing

The following tips can help improve your juicing experience:

● Use the freshest fruits and vegetables to obtain the best tasting and most nutritious juice.

● Make only as much juice as you need right away. With no preservatives, fresh juice begins to lose flavor and nutrients immediately after juicing.

● For best results, select produce that is ripe (or if necessary, nearly ripe) and still on the firm side. Softer pieces do not do as well in centrifugal juicers.

● Wash your hands with soap and warm water immediately prior to working with produce or any other food.

● Always wash all fruits and vegetables thoroughly—even those you intend to peel—before juicing them. Otherwise, debris and bacteria from the surface can be transferred to the flesh within when you cut into or handle it. Use a vegetable brush or other clean, firm-bristled brush, if necessary, to remove embedded dirt.

● Wash and, if necessary, cut, peel or otherwise prepare produce just before putting it into the juicer.

● Cut out any bruised, soft or damaged areas from produce before putting it into the juicer.

● If you're using produce that has a hard, waxy or inedible skin or rind, peel it before juicing. (The individual ingredient profiles that follow indicate when this is necessary or recommended.)

● Large or hard pits, stones or seeds should be removed from produce before it is fed into the juicer.

● When a recipe calls for leafy greens or fresh herbs, try sandwiching them between pieces of more substantial produce or rolling them up into a tight ball before feeding them into the juicer.

● If the flavor of a juice is too intense, try adding more mildly flavored fruits or vegetables or those with a higher water content (celery, for example) to the mix the next time you make it. Doing so should help dilute the overpowering taste.

Once you've made at least some of the recipes in this book and feel more comfortable with the whole juicing process, try doing some experimenting to create your own personalized juice combinations. After all, variety is the spice of life!

Note

For the recipes in this book, 1 serving is 6 to 8 ounces of juice. Keep in mind that the tremendous variation in ingredients (large or small apples or carrots, juicy or not-so-juicy citrus fruit, etc.) as well as the type of juicer you use may give you different results.

Great Juicing Ingredients

The following profiles highlight many of the best and most nutritious options for juicing. In each profile, you'll find information on the ingredient's major nutrients and potential health benefits as well as advice on preparing it for the juicer. The profiles are in alphabetical order for convenient reference. Following the profiles, you'll find an assortment of delectable juice recipes that can help you take advantage of the flavorful, nutritious goodness of the produce. Enjoy!

APPLES

Benefits: Science has given us evidence to support the old adage that "an apple a day keeps the doctor away." Apples and their fresh juice are rich in vitamin C, which is essential to a strong immune system. Frequently including apples into your juice blends may be one of the best things you can do to help your body fight off colds, flu and other illnesses. Apples also contain vitamins A, E and K and the minerals potassium and calcium.

Preparation: Wash apples well under cool running water and twist off the stems. If your juicer can accommodate their size, feed whole apples, unpeeled, into the machine. If not, cut them into halves or quarters first.

APRICOTS

Benefits: Apricots are a great source of beta-carotene, a form of vitamin A that also acts as a powerful antioxidant, meaning that it helps protect cells in the body from damage caused by exposure to unstable oxygen molecules. In addition, the vitamin A activity of beta-carotene helps to protect eyesight. Apricots also offer potassium—which helps the body regulate blood pressure—as well as some calcium and iron.

Preparation: Wash apricots gently but thoroughly in cool running water. Cut the fruit in half and remove the pits.

ASPARAGUS

Benefits: Asparagus can help shield your heart and blood vessels from damage. It provides potassium, a mineral essential for balancing out the sodium in our diets and keeping blood pressure under control. The tall, slender spears also offer two antioxidant vitamins—A, in the form of beta-carotene, and C—that studies suggest can aid in the fight against heart disease.

Preparation: Rinse individual spears thoroughly, use the side of a knife blade or a vegetable peeler to scrape off the tough skin on the lower part of each stalk (the section you'd remove and discard prior to cooking) and trim off any dried-out ends.

BASIL

Benefits: The magnesium in basil can improve blood flow throughout the body by causing blood vessels to relax, a benefit for people who suffer from high blood pressure or hardening of the arteries. Fresh basil also contributes beta-carotene and phytonutrients called flavonoids that are part of the body's natural defenses against damage caused by oxygen—damage that is thought to lead to multiple diseases, including cancer and heart disease.

Preparation: Wash basil thoroughly by swishing it in a bowl of cold water and blotting dry with a paper towel. Roll the sprigs into a ball or sandwich them between more substantial produce, then feed into the juicer.

BEETS

Benefits: Beets are a great source of folic acid, an essential B vitamin that's especially valuable for women of childbearing age because it can help prevent neural-tube birth defects in their offspring. Beets also contain vitamin C, which actually helps to preserve folic acid in addition to being important for a strong immune system. And beets provide potassium, which is important for controlling blood pressure.

Preparation: Wash beets gently to prevent breaks in the skin that will allow the color and nutrients to escape. If you must cut up the beets to fit them in the juicer, consider wearing rubber gloves and an apron to prevent staining your hands and clothes.

Beet Warning

Beets contain substances called oxalates, which can be problematic for people with kidney or gallbladder problems. If you have either, check with your health care provider before including beets in your juices.

BELL PEPPERS

Benefits: Bell peppers contain more Vitamin C than citrus fruits; they also offer a rich store of vitamin A in the form of beta-carotene. Together, these antioxidant nutrients may help defend the body's cells and tissues from damage that can lead to a host of health problems which become more common as we age, such as heart attack, stroke and certain cancers. Bell peppers also contain a phytonutrient called lutein, which may help reduce the risk of the sight-stealing disease macular degeneration.

Preparation: Wash peppers thoroughly under cool running water. Remove the stems and as many seeds as you can and cut into two or three pieces.

BLACKBERRIES

Benefits: The deep, dark color of blackberries results from high levels of anthocyanins, a type of antioxidant phytonutrient that works to defend the body's cells against free radicals (unstable oxygen molecules). Free radical damage contributes to many negative effects, from cataracts and cancerous cells to wrinkles and age spots. Blackberries are also rich in vitamin C and a phytonutrient called ellagic acid, both potent cancer fighters in their own right.

Preparation: Wash berries gently but thoroughly under cool running water.

BLUEBERRIES

Benefits: Blueberries have one of the highest antioxidant contents of any fruit, and those antioxidants appear useful in warding off heart attack, stroke and certain cancers. Some research even suggests that the antioxidant power of blueberries may help protect brain cells and cognitive function and possibly even partially reverse some early memory loss among older adults. Blueberries also supply both iron and vitamin C, a beneficial combination since C enables the body to better absorb iron from plant foods. And like their cousins the cranberries, blueberries can help prevent and treat urinary tract infections.

Preparation: Wash berries gently but thoroughly under cool running water.

BOK CHOY

Benefits: Bok choy's deep green hue advertises its hefty beta-carotene load, meaning it can help the body protect itself from disease-causing damage. This cabbage variety also offers potassium and calcium, minerals that help the body regulate blood pressure. And unlike other nondairy calcium sources, bok choy is low in oxalates, a substance that decreases calcium absorption. Adequate calcium intake is vital for maintaining strong bones and teeth.

Preparation: Remove any cut or browning leaves, then use a sharp knife to cut off the bottom of the plant so the stalks separate. Rinse individual stalks and leaves under cool running water to remove dirt.

BROCCOLI

Benefits: Broccoli is a treasure trove of valuable nutrients, including vitamins C, E and A (mostly as the antioxidant beta-carotene) and minerals such as calcium, folate and potassium. The vitamin C and beta-carotene help shield the body's cells from everyday damage that can lead to disease. The vitamin E not only helps defend the body's tissues but protects other antioxidants. Calcium is important for strong bones throughout life, folate helps prevent certain birth defects and potassium plays a role in warding off stroke.

Preparation: Remove and discard the large woody stem and cut the head into pieces that will fit in the juicer. Rinse the pieces thoroughly under cool running water.

BRUSSELS SPROUTS

Benefits: Brussels sprouts are a good source of protein compared to most other fruits and vegetables, and they're far lower in calories and sodium than animal sources of protein. The vegetable protein is not complete, but it is an essential component of countless body tissues—including your muscles, organs, skin and even hair and nails. Brussels sprouts are also packed with potent phytonutrients and vitamin C, which help protect your body from damage and disease.

Preparation: Rinse brussels sprouts under cool running water, pull off wilted leaves and trim the stem ends.

BUTTERNUT SQUASH

Benefits: The orange-yellow color of this squash shouts beta-carotene, that antioxidant precursor of vitamin A that works to defend the body's tissues from damage caused by exposure to sunlight, toxic fumes, radiation, tobacco smoke and other potentially cancer-causing substances. It also provides decent amounts of vitamin C for a healthy immune system and calcium for strong bones.

Preparation: Use a sharp knife or vegetable peeler to remove the peel, then cut the squash in half lengthwise. Scoop out the seeds and pulp, lay the halves flat side down and cut into pieces that will fit in the juicer.

CABBAGE

Benefits: Both red and green cabbage provide vitamin C, although the red variety has about twice as much as the green. Vitamin C is essential for building and repairing blood vessels, skin and connective tissues such as ligaments and tendons. It also aids in wound healing and keeps the immune system sharp. Red and green cabbage also provide a bit of iron, a mineral essential to healthy red blood cells, which carry oxygen to every cell in the body.

Preparation: Remove and discard loose, bruised or wilted leaves, then rinse the cabbage under cool running water. Cut the head in half, lay each half flat side down and cut into wedges.

CANTALOUPE

Benefits: If you want to arm your body with some of the best weapons for fighting heart disease, cancer, infections and more, cantaloupe is a sure bet. This sweet, juicy melon is rich in the cell-defending antioxidant beta-carotene, immunity-boosting vitamin C, and disease-fighting phytonutrients. It's also a good source of potassium, which helps the body get rid of excess sodium; excess sodium can contribute to high blood pressure and stroke risk in susceptible individuals.

Preparation: Hold the cantaloupe under cool running water and use a vegetable brush to scrub the netted surface clean. Cut the melon in half and scoop out the stringy seeds, then cut the halves into wedges and remove the rind.

CARROTS

Benefits: It's no myth: Carrots really are good for eyesight. The abundant vitamin A, in the form of beta-carotene, helps protect the eyes from vision stealers like night blindness, cataracts and macular degeneration. Vitamin A also helps to keep the body's outer shield—the skin—supple and strong.

Preparation: Wash carrots under cool running water, using a stiff-bristled vegetable brush to remove dirt and debris.

Keep Carrots Handy

Carrot juice, like apple juice, is tasty on its own but also makes a great base for juice combinations that include a variety of other vegetables and fruits.

CAULIFLOWER

Benefits: You might think cauliflower's pale color means it's low in health-promoting constituents, but cauliflower comes in second only to citrus fruits in vitamin C content. Research suggests vitamin C may help defend blood vessels from damage and possibly slow the hardening of arteries that can lead to heart attack and stroke. Plus, the natural chemical that gives cauliflower its sharp taste may help fight cancers of the breast and prostate.

Preparation: Remove outer leaves, trim brown spots, break into florets and wash under cool running water.

CELERY

Benefits: Despite the fact that it is mostly water, celery supplies essential vitamins A, C and K as well as the minerals folic acid, which can help prevent certain birth birth defects, and potassium, which helps regulate blood pressure. Celery also contains phytonutrients called phthalides, which recent research suggests may help protect the brain from oxidative stress and so may prove useful in keeping diseases such as Alzheimer's and Parkinson's at bay.

Preparation: Separate into stalks, trim the greens and any dried-out ends, and wash the stalks well under cool running water.

CHERRIES

Benefits: Both sweet and tart (sour) cherries provide disease-fighting antioxidants such as beta-carotene and vitamin C, which help defend the body's cells from damage. Both also offer potassium, the mineral that helps the body get rid of excess sodium. But tart cherries actually pack more nutrients. Recent research also suggests tart cherries can help fight inflammation, which can be beneficial in various ways, from easing arthritis pain and muscle soreness to potentially lowering the risk of heart disease.

Preparation: Remove the stems, then wash cherries thoroughly under cool running water and remove the pits.

CHILE PEPPERS

Benefits: Early research suggests capsaicin, the substance that gives chiles their characteristic bite, may help improve insulin's ability to lower blood sugar after meals. If these findings are confirmed, chile peppers could prove a useful tool in helping to prevent and treat type 2 diabetes. Chile peppers are also rich in beta-carotene and vitamin C, two antioxidants that can help prevent heart disease, cancer and other chronic diseases.

Preparation: Wash chile peppers well under cool running water. Wear gloves and avoid touching your eyes when handling chile peppers, and wash your hands, utensils and cutting board with soap and water afterwards. Cut off the stem end, slice the pepper down the center and feed pieces into the juicer. (If you prefer a less spicy juice, remove and discard the seeds and fiery white membrane.)

CILANTRO

Benefits: Fresh cilantro provides vitamin K, which is essential for proper blood clotting, as well as the minerals iron, magnesium and manganese. Iron is vital for healthy red blood cells, which transport oxygen to the body's cells; magnesium and manganese are important for proper metabolism. Fresh cilantro also contains phytonutrients that may help protect us against cancer.

Preparation: Discard any yellowed or wilted leaves and wash the cilantro under cool running water. Blot dry with a paper towel and either roll sprigs into a tight ball or place them between pieces of firmer produce and feed them into the juicer.

COCONUT WATER

Found inside young, green coconuts, coconut water is a clear liquid with a sweet, coconutty flavor. It should not be confused with white-colored coconut milk, which is pressed from the meat of mature coconuts. Unlike coconut meat and milk, coconut water is low in calories and fat free, so it's a healthier way to add coconut flavor to your juice. It is also rich in electrolytes, such as potassium, making it great for rehydration. Since immature coconuts are not readily available in most U.S. grocery stores, you'll need to purchase prepackaged coconut water to add to your juices.

CRANBERRIES

Benefits: Phytonutrients in cranberries prevent certain bacteria from sticking to the walls of the urinary tract, thus helping to prevent and treat urinary tract infections and interstitial cystitis (a condition causing bladder and pelvic discomfort). The same antibacterial action may also help to prevent gum disease and stomach ulcers, which are commonly caused by bacteria. Cranberries also offer phytonutrients that can help protect against disease of the heart and eyes.

Preparation: Wash cranberries thoroughly under cool running water, removing any shriveled or bruised berries.

CUCUMBERS

Benefits: Although cucumbers are mostly water, they do provide a decent dose of potassium, the essential mineral that's important for muscle contraction, nerve transmission, fluid balance and proper functioning of the heart and kidneys.

Preparation: Wash cucumbers thoroughly under cool running water. Tougher-skinned varieties should be peeled prior to juicing; softer-skinned cukes may simply need to be cut up to fit in the juicer.

CURRANTS

Benefits: Both black and red currants pack plenty of vitamin C, which helps keep the immune system functioning well. Red currants are also rich in antioxidants that help protect the body's cells from damage caused by unstable oxygen molecules, the kind of damage that can lead to heart disease, cancer and other health problems. Black currants are a good source of two essential minerals: manganese, which is important for bone structure, and potassium, which plays many roles, including helping to regulate body fluids and blood pressure.

Preparation: Wash currants thoroughly under cool running water.

FENNEL

Benefits: Low-calorie fennel offers vitamin C for a healthy immune system; calcium for strong bones; iron for plentiful red blood cells, which deliver life-sustaining oxygen to all the cells of the body; folate to help prevent neural tube birth defects; and potassium to balance out the sodium in our diets and keep blood pressure in check.

Preparation: Rinse fennel thoroughly under cool running water, making sure to remove dirt from the bulb and between the stalks. If necessary, cut the bulb into pieces that will fit in the juicer.

GARLIC

Benefits: Much of garlic's healing power appears to stem from allicin, the compound that makes the bulb so pungent when crushed, chopped or cooked. Studies suggest garlic can aid in lowering blood pressure and slowing the clogging of arteries that can lead to heart attack and stroke. It appears to have some anti-cancer effects, as well. Garlic also thins the blood (so if you consume a lot of it, alert your doctor before having any kind of surgery) and appears to have antibacterial and antiviral properties.

Preparation: Peel the desired number of cloves and feed them into the juicer with larger pieces of produce.

GINGER

Benefits: Research indicates that ginger is helpful for relieving the symptoms of motion sickness, morning sickness during pregnancy and nausea associated with chemotherapy. Indeed, ginger has been valued for its digestion-soothing effects for centuries. It's also filled with phytonutrients that act against inflammation, which may help explain its apparent ability to reduce joint pain, swelling and stiffness in people with arthritis. Ginger's anti-inflammatory actions may also prove beneficial for combatting cancer, heart disease and the growing list of other diseases that are being linked to chronic inflammation in the body.

Preparation: Use a sharp knife to peel off the tough skin that encases the entire root. If you purchase young ginger with very thin skin, no peeling is necessary.

GRAPEFRUIT

Benefits: Grapefruit is packed with vitamin C, and the pink and red varieties also offer plentiful vitamin A in the form of beta-carotene. These vitamins, along with another antioxidant phytonutrient called lycopene, help protect cells from the type of everyday damage that can lead to cancer and other chronic diseases. Grapefruit also contains phytonutrients that protect against certain types of eye disease.

Preparation: Wash under cool running water and remove the peel.

Grapefruit Warning

Grapefruit and its juice can interfere with the actions of certain prescription drugs, so if you take medication, check the label or consult your doctor or pharmacist to find out if you can safely enjoy this refreshing juice.

GRAPES

Benefits: Grapes, especially the red and purple varieties, contain powerful health-preserving phytonutrients that have shown promise in fighting cancer and lowering the risk of heart disease and stroke by reducing potentially damaging blood clots, improving blood flow and interfering with the process that deposits cholesterol on artery walls. Although much of the phytonutrient content is in the skins, the heat produced during the juicing process may help transfer some of that content to the juice.

Preparation: Wash grapes under cool running water and remove them from their stems.

GREEN BEANS

Benefits: Green beans are rich in carotenoids, including lutein for healthy vision and beta-carotene for protection against cell damage from unstable oxygen molecules, which can lead to cancer and other chronic diseases. They also supply calcium and phosphorus, two minerals necessary for healthy bones and teeth.

Preparation: Wash green beans under cool running water.

GREENS

Benefits: Leafy greens—such as beet, turnip, collard, mustard and dandelion—have more antioxidants than many other fruits and vegetables, meaning they can help protect the cells in your body from damage. They also provide calcium, which is important for strong bones and teeth as well as proper muscle function and the transmission of impulses through the nerves.

Preparation: Wash greens well under cool running water and discard tough stems. Roll greens into a ball or place them between firm produce to feed them into the juicer.

HONEY

Honey appears to have some mild antibacterial and antioxidant properties; darker honeys may contain more of these. Some research also suggests that honey may help calm coughs and soothe irritated mucous membranes, such as those lining the throat.

HONEYDEW

Benefits: Honeydew melon is an excellent source of vitamin C, which is essential for the formation and repair of collagen, a type of tissue that holds the body's cells and tissues together and is a primary component of blood vessels. Vitamin C also promotes the normal development of bones and teeth. Honeydew provides some calcium, which helps keep bones and teeth strong, and iron, which is needed to transport oxygen to the body's cells.

Preparation: Wash the melon under cool running water, using a vegetable brush to scrub the rind. Cut the melon in half and scoop out the stringy seeds, then cut the halves into wedges and remove the rind.

JICAMA

Benefits: Low-calorie, low-sodium jicama is an excellent source of vitamin C, which helps fuel your immune system; promotes healthy bones, teeth and gums; and helps protect blood vessels from damage that can lead to heart attack or stroke.

Preparation: Wash jicama under cool running water, using a vegetable brush to clean the skin. Cut into large pieces, if necessary.

KALE

Benefits: Kale stands a head above other greens as an excellent source of beta-carotene and vitamin C, two antioxidants believed to be major players in the body's battle against cancer, heart disease and certain age-related declines in vision and cognitive function. Kale is packed with readily absorbed calcium, a mineral that is vital to warding off the bone-thinning disease osteoporosis and may also help keep blood pressure in a healthy range. Kale also provides decent amounts of folate, iron and potassium.

Preparation: Wash kale thoroughly under cool running water to remove dirt and sand from the leaves, and remove any tough center stems. Roll the leaves into a ball or slip them between firmer pieces of produce to feed them into the juicer.

KIWI

Benefits: One medium kiwi provides an entire day's worth of vitamin C, which not only helps maintain a strong immune system and healthy teeth and gums but may protect the arteries—including those feeding the heart and brain—from damage. Kiwi also packs potassium for healthy blood pressure and the antioxidants lutein and zeaxanthin, which safeguard eye health.

Preparation: Wash kiwi under cool running water and remove the peel. Cut into smaller pieces, if necessary.

LEMONS

Benefits: Lemons are loaded with vitamin C, a nutrient the body needs to heal wounds and perform all sorts of daily maintenance. For example, vitamin C is required for making collagen, a protein the body uses to grow and repair blood vessels, skin, cartilage, ligaments, tendons and bones. Vitamin C also helps ward off inflammation, heart disease and cancer.

Preparation: Wash lemons well under cool running water and remove the peel.

LIMES

Benefits: In addition to packing a powerful vitamin C punch, limes are full of an antioxidant phytochemical called limonin, which has shown anticancer, anti-inflammatory, antiviral and cholesterol-lowering effects in laboratory tests.

Preparation: Wash limes well under cool running water and remove the peel.

MANGOES

Benefits: Mangoes are a superior source of beta-carotene, a vitamin A precursor and antioxidant linked to a reduced risk of some forms of cancer. And a single mango offers nearly a full day's supply of vitamin C, a powerful antioxidant and important player in the body's ability to prevent infection. Mangoes also contribute calcium, potassium and magnesium, and regularly consuming foods rich in these minerals is associated with lower blood pressure.

Preparation: Wash mangoes thoroughly under cool running water before removing the peel and large pits.

MINT

Benefits: Mints, including the familiar peppermint and spearmint, offer vitamin C and beta-carotene, both of which have disease-fighting antioxidant actions. They also supply manganese, which is necessary for the body to properly metabolize carbohydrates and fats. In addition, a phytonutrient in mint appears to help block production of leukotrienes, molecules that trigger inflammation in the nasal passages, causing stuffiness. And the oil within the peppermint plant has a long history of helping to calm intestinal cramping and other discomforts of the digestive tract.

Preparation: Wash mint thoroughly by swishing it in a bowl of cold water, then blot it dry with a paper towel. Roll the sprigs into a ball or sandwich them between more substantial produce, and feed into the juicer.

ONIONS

Benefits: Onions provide some of the same heart- and brain-protecting effects as their cousin garlic does. They appear to help reduce blood clotting and lower damaging levels of cholesterol in the blood, which together can help prevent the narrowing and eventual blockage of arteries that can lead to heart attack and stroke. They also supply phytonutrients that fight inflammation, which many experts believe is a contributing factor in a host of chronic diseases, from cancer and heart disease to arthritis, asthma and type 2 diabetes. One such phytonutrient, quercetin, may help relieve chronic inflammation of the prostate and possibly even help fight allergies.

Preparation: Remove the papery skin, wash under cool running water and cut into pieces that will fit in the juicer.

ORANGES

Benefits: A single orange packs more than a day's worth of your vitamin C requirement. This antioxidant vitamin helps protect tissues and organs from damage; fuels immune function to protect us against infections; and plays a role in maintaining healthy blood vessels, bones, teeth and gums. The folate in oranges is important for women in their childbearing years as it helps prevent certain birth defects. And the plentiful potassium is beneficial for keeping blood pressure under control.

Preparation: Wash oranges well under cool running water and remove the peel.

PAPAYA

Benefits: Papayas pack plenty of potassium, a mineral that's essential for proper fluid balance, blood-pressure regulation and the health of your kidneys. As you might guess from their vibrant orange flesh, papayas are also loaded with the beta-carotene form of vitamin A as well as plenty of vitamin C, both of which help fight cancer and heart disease.

Preparation: Wash the papaya well under cool running water. Cut it in half lengthwise and use a spoon to scoop out the seeds. Cut it into pieces that will fit in the juicer.

PARSLEY

Benefits: Parsley is good for more than freshening your breath with its chlorophyll. Early research suggests it may have some benefit in lowering blood sugar, which is promising news for people with diabetes. Parsley also contains powerful phytonutrients called flavonoids, along with beta-carotene and vitamin C, which may help protect blood vessels from inflammation and damage that can lead to vision loss, heart attack and stroke.

Preparation: Wash parsley thoroughly by swishing it in a bowl of cold water, then blot it dry with a paper towel. Roll the sprigs into a ball or sandwich them between more substantial produce, and feed into the juicer.

PARSNIPS

Benefits: Parsnips are a good source of folate, an essential B vitamin the body needs to form oxygen-carrying red blood cells. Folate also appears to help lower the risk of heart disease and can help women of childbearing age prevent certain birth defects in their offspring. Parsnips supply ample amounts of potassium, which is needed to regulate blood pressure.

Preparation: Wash parsnips under cool running water, using a stiff-bristled vegetable brush to remove dirt and debris.

PEACHES

Benefits: Peaches are a sweet and low-calorie source of nutrients that can help protect the body from damage that can lead to chronic disease. But peaches and other produce that contain similar nutrients may be especially beneficial for people with diabetes, because the beta-carotene and vitamin C in the fruit may help prevent or delay some of the complications of diabetes, such as nerve damage and vision loss. Peaches are also a rich source of potassium, an essential mineral that can help keep blood pressure in a healthy range.

Preparation: Wash peaches gently but thoroughly in cool running water. Cut the fruit in half and remove the pits.

PEARS

Benefits: Pears provide vitamin C and the mineral copper, which work as antioxidants in the body to help protect cells, tissues and organs from damage caused by unstable molecules called free radicals. Pears also supply both calcium and boron, essential minerals important to bone health. Calcium is required for building and maintaining bone, and boron helps the body use the calcium it takes in.

Preparation: Remove the stems, wash the pears thoroughly under cool running water and, if necessary, cut them in half to fit in the juicer.

PINEAPPLE

Benefits: Pineapples are virtually dripping with vitamin C, the antioxidant that's also essential for keeping your immune system revved up to resist colds, flu and other infections. On top of that, a cup of pineapple supplies more than the recommended daily intake of manganese, an essential mineral that plays a role in energy production and helps keep bones strong. This tropical treat also offers decent amounts of copper, for proper brain and nerve function, and folate, which can help prevent certain birth defects. Fresh, raw pineapple contains the enzyme bromelain, a digestive aid that helps prevent inflammation and swelling, too.

Preparation: Wash the pineapple and use a vegetable brush to scrub the skin. Cut a small slice from the bottom and cut off the top of the fruit. Stand the pineapple on a cutting board and use a sharp knife to cut away the skin. Remove any remaining eyes with the tip of a knife or vegetable peeler and cut the whole peeled pineapple into quarters.

PLUMS

Benefits: Plums provide vitamins A and C as well as potassium. The vitamins are cell defenders that can help keep chronic disease at bay, while potassium is important for fluid balance, blood pressure regulation and a steady heartbeat.

Preparation: Wash plums gently but thoroughly in cool running water. Cut the fruit in half and remove the pits.

POMEGRANATES

Benefits: Pomegranates are truly a heart's delight. They supply a rich dose of potassium for maintaining a steady heartbeat and healthy blood pressure. Their juice is full of heart-protective antioxidants, with nearly three times the antioxidant content of red wine or green tea. Pomegranate juice may also help reduce the buildup and lower blood levels of artery-clogging cholesterol and improve blood flow.

Preparation: Wash pomegranates well under cool running water, then cut into pieces. (The juice can stain, so consider wearing gloves and an apron.) Immerse the pieces in a bowl of cold water to pry off the seeds. The membrane that holds the seeds in place will float to the top; it has a bitter taste, so discard it. Collect the seeds and feed them into the juicer. For convenience, you can find containers of ready-to-use pomegranate seeds in the refrigerated produce section of some supermarkets.

RADISHES

Benefits: Radishes offer calcium for strong bones and teeth; potassium for a steady heartbeat and lower blood pressure; iron for plenty of oxygen-carrying red blood cells; selenium for healthy hair, nails and muscles; and magnesium for proper nerve, muscle and immune function.

Preparation: Wash radishes under cool running water, using a vegetable brush to scrub away stuck-on dirt, if necessary.

RASPBERRIES

Benefits: Raspberries are an amazingly compact and delicious source of a slew of beneficial nutrients, including free radical-fighting vitamins A, C and E; essential minerals, including copper, iron, magnesium, manganese and potassium; and health-promoting phytochemicals, including phenolic compounds that have shown promise in battling cancer, inflammation (which may be behind a variety of chronic diseases, including heart disease) and degenerative nerve diseases, such as Alzheimer's.

Preparation: Wash berries gently but thoroughly under cool running water.

SPINACH

Benefits: Spinach has an incredibly rich and potent mix of essential nutrients with antioxidant functions, including vitamins A, C and E and the minerals manganese, selenium and zinc. Spinach also provides more than a dozen antioxidant and anti-inflammatory phytonutrients, making it helpful in fighting high blood pressure; hardening of the arteries and stroke; various cancers; and age-related eye diseases such as cataracts and macular degeneration. Spinach also contributes iron and folic acid for healthy oxygen-carrying red blood cells.

Preparation: Wash spinach leaves well under cool running water and discard tough stems. Roll the leaves into a ball or place them between firm produce to feed them into the juicer.

SPROUTS

Benefits: Sprouts are concentrated sources of several essential nutrients, including the antioxidant vitamin C and vitamin K, which plays an important role in proper blood clotting. Sprouts also contribute iron, for healthy red blood cells, and folate, which can help prevent certain birth defects when consumed in sufficient amount by women in their childbearing years.

Preparation: Place the sprouts in a colander under cool running water for at least two minutes, using your fingers to toss them like a salad so that they are thoroughly rinsed. Lay them on paper towels, cover with more paper towels and blot them dry. Wad up the sprouts or place them between pieces of other produce to feed them into the juicer.

STRAWBERRIES

Benefits: Strawberries contain a phytonutrient called ellagic acid that helps fight inflammation and cancer-causing cell damage. They're also a top source of immunity-boosting vitamin C, containing more of this antioxidant than oranges. Strawberries also supply lots of potassium, which helps the body regulate blood pressure and so may help prevent stroke.

Preparation: Wash berries well under cool running water and remove the green tops.

SWEET POTATOES

Benefits: Sweet potatoes provide a jaw-dropping amount of vitamin A in the form of antioxidant beta-carotene, making them an incredibly valuable tool in warding off chronic diseases such as cancer and heart disease, as well as diseases such as asthma and rheumatoid arthritis that involve inflammation. Sweet potatoes also pack a powerful vitamin C punch and a hefty load of potassium.

Preparation: Wash sweet potatoes under cool running water, using a vegetable brush to remove dirt and debris. If necessary, cut them into pieces that will fit in the juicer.

SWISS CHARD

Benefits: Swiss chard is loaded with antioxidant nutrients, including vitamins A and C, which help protect the body's cells from inflammation and damage caused by exposure to unstable oxygen molecules within the body and toxic substances from the environment. Swiss chard also contains phytonutrients that may help control blood sugar in people with type 2 diabetes.

Preparation: Wash Swiss chard under cool running water. Stack the leaves, roll them into a ball or bundle and feed them into the juicer.

TANGERINES

Benefits: Sweet, low-calorie tangerines are loaded with vitamin A in the form of beta-carotene, which can help prevent night blindness and protect the cells in the eyes and the rest of the body from damage caused by ultraviolet light, radiation, air pollution, cigarette smoke and other toxic substances. Tangerines also supply calcium, a mineral essential to strong bones and teeth and a steady heart rate.

Preparation: Wash tangerines under cool running water and remove the peel.

TOMATOES

Benefits: Research suggests that lycopene, the phytonutrient that gives tomatoes their red hue, may help reduce the risk of heart and blood vessel disease as well as prostate cancer. The carotenoids, including beta-carotene, are also powerful weapons against cardiovascular disease, cancer and other chronic ailments. Tomatoes also provide vitamin C for a strong immune system and potassium for healthy blood pressure.

Preparation: Wash tomatoes well under cool running water and remove any stems. If necessary, cut into halves or quarters.

TURNIPS

Benefits: Turnips contain lysine, an amino acid that's useful in preventing and treating cold sores. They also have some vitamin C, which the immune system needs to fight viruses, bacteria and other infectious agents. And turnips supply the minerals potassium and calcium, which work to keep blood pressure in a healthy range.

Preparation: Wash turnips well under cool running water; use a vegetable brush to remove stubborn dirt. Small turnips can go in the juicer unpeeled; larger turnips should be peeled and, if necessary, cut into smaller pieces before being fed into the juicer.

WATERCRESS

Benefits: Like its cruciferous cousins, including broccoli, cabbage and kale, watercress is rich in antioxidants, including beta-carotene and lutein, which help protect the eyes from damage and combat the deleterious effects of free radicals that can lead to the development and growth of cancer cells. Watercress has also been found to contain phytonutrients that aid detoxification and help protect the lungs from cancerous changes. Watercress also offers calcium and potassium, which are essential for a healthy heart.

Preparation: Rinse the leaves thoroughly under cool running water and pat them

dry with a paper towel. Roll them into a ball or slip them between firm pieces of produce and feed them into the juicer.

WATERMELON

Benefits: Unlike other melons, watermelon is a valuable source of lycopene, the phytonutrient responsible for tomatoes' red hue. Research has shown that lycopene can reduce the risk of cancers of the breast, colon and prostate. Watermelon also provides disease-fighting antioxidants vitamin C and beta-carotene. And it offers a decent dose of potassium, which helps keep blood pressure in a healthy range and may reduce the risk of kidney stones and perhaps even bone loss.

Preparation: Wash the watermelon thoroughly under cool running water, then use a sharp knife to cut it into smaller pieces and remove the rind.

ZUCCHINI

Benefits: Zucchini provides the mineral folate along with vitamins A and C, all of which help to protect the cells in the heart and other parts of the body from damage that can lead to disease. Zucchini's potassium adds to the cardiovascular benefit of the vegetable by helping the body maintain a steady heartbeat and healthy blood pressure.

Preparation: Wash zucchini well under cool running water and, if the peel is waxy, remove the peel. (Removing the peel will also produce a milder-tasting juice.)

Apples

Mean and Green

1 green apple
2 stalks celery
3 leaves kale
½ cucumber
½ lemon, peeled
1 inch fresh ginger, peeled

Juice apple, celery, kale, cucumber, lemon and ginger. Stir.

Makes 2 servings

Really Rhubarb

3 apples
2 stalks rhubarb

Juice apples and rhubarb. Stir.

Makes 2 servings

Mean and Green

Apples

Orchard Crush

2 apples
1 cup raspberries
1 cup strawberries

Juice apples, raspberries and strawberries. Stir.   *Makes 2 servings*

Spicy Apple Peach

2 apples
8 leaves mustard greens
2 stalks celery
1 kiwi, peeled
1 peach

Juice apples, mustard greens, celery, kiwi and peach. Stir.

Makes 2 servings

Orchard Crush

Apples

Tangerapple

2 apples
2 tangerines, peeled
¼ lemon, peeled

Juice apples, tangerines and lemon. Stir.

Makes 2 servings

Sharp Apple Cooler

3 apples
1 cucumber
¼ cup fresh mint
1 inch fresh ginger, peeled

Juice apples, cucumber, mint and ginger. Stir.

Makes 2 servings

Tangerapple

Apricots

Orange Apricot

6 apricots
1 orange, peeled
Ice cubes

Juice apricots and orange. Stir. Serve over ice.   *Makes 2 servings*

Star of the Show

2 apricots
2 plums
¼ pineapple, peeled
1 peach
1 star fruit

Juice apricots, plums, pineapple, peach and star fruit. Stir.

Makes 2 servings

Orange Apricot

Asparagus

Spring Green Cocktail

8 spears asparagus
1 cucumber
1 tomato
½ lemon, peeled

Juice asparagus, cucumber, tomato and lemon. Stir.

Makes 2 servings

Arthritis Tonic

4 spears asparagus
3 carrots
3 stalks celery
1 apple
1 cup broccoli florets
1 cup fresh parsley

Juice asparagus, carrots, celery, apple, broccoli and parsley. Stir.

Makes 2 servings

32

Spring Green Cocktail

Basil

Cucumber Basil Cooler

    1 cucumber
    1 apple
    ½ cup fresh basil
    ½ lime, peeled

Juice cucumber, apple, basil and lime. Stir.   *Makes 2 servings*

Tangy Tomato Basil

    2 tomatoes
    1 cup fresh spinach
    4 sprigs fresh basil
    ½ lemon, peeled

Juice tomatoes, spinach, basil and lemon. Stir.   *Makes 2 servings*

Cucumber Basil Cooler

Beets

Purple Pineapple Juice

1 beet
1 pear
¼ pineapple, peeled
1 inch fresh ginger, peeled

Juice beet, pear, pineapple and ginger. Stir.   *Makes 2 servings*

Early Riser Breakfast

1 beet
¼ red cabbage
2 carrots
½ red bell pepper
1 orange, peeled
1 apple
½ lemon, peeled

Juice beet, cabbage, carrots, bell pepper, orange, apple and lemon.
Stir.   *Makes 2 servings*

Beets

Ruby Apple Stinger

2 beets
2 carrots
½ apple
1 inch fresh ginger, peeled
¼ lemon, peeled

Juice beets, carrots, apple, ginger and lemon. Stir.   *Makes 2 servings*

Veggie Chiller

3 carrots
1 beet
½ sweet potato
¼ bulb fennel

Juice carrots, beet, sweet potato and fennel. Stir.   *Makes 2 servings*

Ruby Apple Stinger

Bell Peppers

Triple Pepper

2 apples
1 red bell pepper
1 yellow bell pepper
½ jalapeño pepper

Juice apples, bell peppers and jalapeño pepper. Stir.

Makes 2 servings

Rabbit Juice

½ green cabbage
1 red bell pepper
1 tomato
¼ cup fresh parsley

Juice cabbage, bell pepper, tomato and parsley. Stir.

Makes 2 servings

Blackberries

Super Berry Refresher

- 1 cup strawberries
- 1 cup raspberries
- 1 cucumber
- ½ cup blackberries
- ½ cup blueberries
- ¼ lemon, peeled

Juice strawberries, raspberries, cucumber, blackberries, blueberries and lemon. Stir.

Makes 2 servings

Kale & Fruit Juice

- 2 apples
- 2 carrots
- 1 orange, peeled
- 1 cup blackberries
- 3 leaves kale

Juice apples, carrots, orange, blackberries and kale. Stir.

Makes 2 servings

Super Berry Refresher

Blueberries

Blueberry Haze

2 apples
1 ½ cups blueberries
½ grapefruit, peeled
1 inch fresh ginger, peeled

Juice apples, blueberries, grapefruit and ginger. Stir.   *Makes 2 servings*

Green Berry Booster

1 cup blueberries
1 cucumber
1 apple
4 leaves collard greens, Swiss chard or kale
½ lemon, peeled

Juice blueberries, cucumber, apple, collard greens and lemon. Stir.
Makes 2 servings

44

Bok Choy

Cleansing Green Juice

4 leaves bok choy
1 stalk celery
½ cucumber
¼ bulb fennel
½ lemon, peeled

Juice bok choy, celery, cucumber, fennel and lemon. Stir.

Makes 2 servings

Super Beta-Carotene

4 carrots
1 apple
4 leaves bok choy
2 leaves kale
½ inch fresh ginger, peeled

Juice carrots, apple, bok choy, kale and ginger. Stir.   *Makes 2 servings*

Cleansing Green Juice

Broccoli

Sweet & Green

1 cup broccoli florets
¼ pineapple, peeled
2 stalks celery

Juice broccoli, pineapple and celery. Stir.   *Makes 2 servings*

Drinkable Slaw

2 cups broccoli florets
½ small red cabbage
2 carrots
1 apple
½ lemon, peeled
½ inch fresh ginger, peeled

Juice broccoli, cabbage, carrots, apple, lemon and ginger. Stir.

Makes 2 servings

Sweet & Green

Brussels Sprouts

Citrus Sprout

1 cup brussels sprouts
4 leaves romaine lettuce
1 orange, peeled
½ apple
½ lemon, peeled

Juice brussels sprouts, romaine, orange, apple and lemon. Stir.

Makes 2 servings

Drink a Rainbow

4 carrots
½ pineapple, peeled
2 apples
2 pears
1 beet
½ cup brussels sprouts
½ cup broccoli florets
¼ cup cauliflower florets

Juice carrots, pineapple, apples, pears, beet, brussels sprouts, broccoli and cauliflower. Stir.

Makes 6 servings

Butternut Squash

Autumn Apple Pie Juice

2 apples
½ butternut squash, peeled
¼ teaspoon pumpkin pie spice

Juice apples and squash. Stir in pumpkin pie spice until well blended.

Makes 2 servings

Butternut Sparkler

1 cup cut-up peeled butternut squash
1 carrot
½ pomegranate, peeled
Sparkling water

Juice squash, carrot and pomegranate seeds. Stir. Top with sparkling water.

Makes 2 servings

Autumn Apple Pie Juice

Cabbage

Red Cabbage & Pineapple

¼ **red cabbage**
¼ **pineapple, peeled**

Juice cabbage and pineapple. Stir.

Makes 2 servings

Cabbage Patch Juice

 2 **apples**
¼ **napa cabbage**
¼ **red cabbage**

Juice apples, napa cabbage and red cabbage. Stir.

Makes 2 servings

54

Red Cabbage & Pineapple

Cabbage

Pear Cabbage Juice

¼ **red cabbage**
1 **Asian pear**
1 **apple**
1 **carrot**
½ **lime, peeled**
½ **inch fresh ginger, peeled**

Juice cabbage, pear, apple, carrot, lime and ginger. Stir.

Makes 2 servings

Crimson Carrot

½ **red cabbage**
2 **apples**
1 **carrot**
⅓ **cup red seedless grapes**
Ice cubes

Juice cabbage, apples, carrot and grapes. Stir. Serve over ice.

Makes 2 servings

Cantaloupe

Cantaloupe Ginger

½ **cantaloupe, rind removed**
1 **inch fresh ginger, peeled**

Juice cantaloupe and ginger. Stir.   *Makes 2 servings*

Vitamin Blast

¼ **cantaloupe, rind removed**
1 **orange, peeled**
¼ **papaya**
2 **leaves Swiss chard**

Juice cantaloupe, orange, papaya and chard. Stir.   *Makes 2 servings*

Cantaloupe

Melon Refresher

¼ **cantaloupe, rind removed**
1 **pear**
1 **lime, peeled**
2 **sprigs fresh mint**

Juice cantaloupe, pear, lime and mint. Stir.   *Makes 2 servings*

Cantaloupe & Grape

¼ **cantaloupe, rind removed**
¾ **cup black seedless grapes**
½ **lemon, peeled**

Juice cantaloupe, grapes and lemon. Stir.   *Makes 2 servings*

Melon Refresher

Carrots

Apple Carrot Zinger

4 carrots

2 apples

¼ cucumber

1 inch fresh ginger, peeled

Juice carrots, apples, cucumber and ginger. Stir. *Makes 2 servings*

Healthy Complexion Combo

3 carrots

1 tomato

1 cucumber

½ cup broccoli florets

½ cup watercress

Juice carrots, tomato, cucumber, broccoli and watercress. Stir.

Makes 2 servings

Carrots

Sweet Pepper Carrot

3 carrots
1 red bell pepper
1 yellow bell pepper

Juice carrots and bell peppers. Stir.

Makes 2 servings

Carotene with a Kick

2 carrots
1 apple
1 cup radicchio
4 leaves Swiss chard
2 radishes
½ lime, peeled

Juice carrots, apple, radicchio, chard, radishes and lime. Stir.

Makes 2 servings

Sweet Pepper Carrot

Cauliflower

Headache Buster

1 cup cauliflower florets
1 cup broccoli florets
1 apple

Juice cauliflower, broccoli and apple. Stir.   *Makes 1 serving*

Tomato with a Twist

1 tomato
½ cup cauliflower florets
3 leaves red lettuce
Juice tomato, cauliflower and lettuce. Stir.   *Makes 1 serving*

Headache Buster

Celery

Sweet Celery

3 stalks celery
1 apple
1 lemon, peeled
¼ cup raspberries

Juice celery, apple, lemon and raspberries. Stir.   *Makes 2 servings*

Bedtime Cocktail

½ head romaine lettuce
2 stalks celery
½ cucumber

Juice romaine, celery and cucumber. Stir.   *Makes 2 servings*

Sweet Celery

Celery

Green Energy

   2 stalks celery
   2 apples
   6 leaves kale
   ½ cup fresh spinach
   ½ cucumber
   ¼ bulb fennel
   ½ lemon, peeled
   1 inch fresh ginger, peeled

Juice celery, apples, kale, spinach, cucumber, fennel, lemon and ginger.
Stir.   *Makes 4 servings*

Celery Root-Beet-Carrot Juice

   4 carrots
   1 apple
   1 beet
   ½ celery root, peeled
   ¼ inch fresh ginger, peeled

Juice carrots, apple, beet, celery root and ginger. Stir.

Makes 2 servings

Cherries

Cherry & Melon

⅛ **seedless watermelon, rind removed**
¼ **cantaloupe, rind removed**
¾ **cup cherries, pitted**

Juice watermelon, cantaloupe and cherries. Stir.   *Makes 3 servings*

Cherry Green

1 **cup cherries, pitted**
2 **stalks celery**
1 **apple**
1 **cup fresh parsley**
1 **lemon, peeled**

Juice cherries, celery, apple, parsley and lemon. Stir.

Makes 2 servings

Cherry & Melon

Chile Peppers

Fiery Cucumber Beet Juice

1 cucumber

1 beet

1 lemon, peeled

1 inch fresh ginger, peeled

½ jalapeño pepper

Juice cucumber, beet, lemon, ginger and jalapeño pepper. Stir.

Makes 2 servings

Hotsy Totsy

4 carrots

¼ pineapple, peeled

½ lime, peeled

½ small chile pepper

2 sprigs fresh cilantro

Ice cubes

Juice carrots, pineapple, lime, chile pepper and cilantro. Stir.
Serve over ice.

Makes 2 servings

Fiery Cucumber Beet Juice

Cilantro

Green Queen

1 cup fresh spinach

2 stalks celery

5 leaves kale

1 cup fresh cilantro

½ cucumber

½ apple

½ lemon, peeled

½ inch fresh ginger, peeled

Juice spinach, celery, kale, cilantro, cucumber, apple, lemon and ginger. Stir. *Makes 2 servings*

Veggie Blast

3 stalks celery

1 beet

1 carrot

1 red bell pepper

1 apple

6 leaves kale

½ cup fresh cilantro

1 inch fresh ginger, peeled

¼ teaspoon turmeric

Juice celery, beet, carrot, bell pepper, apple, kale, cilantro and ginger. Stir in turmeric until well blended. *Makes 2 servings*

Coconut Water

Tropical Fruit Fling

¼ **pineapple, peeled**
1 **orange, peeled**
½ **mango, peeled**
½ **cup strawberries**
½ **cup coconut water**

Juice pineapple, orange, mango and strawberries. Stir in coconut water until well blended. *Makes 2 servings*

Tongue Twister

2 **apples**
1½ **cups arugula**
½ **cup fresh cilantro**
½ **jalapeño pepper**
1 **cup coconut water**

Juice apples, arugula, cilantro and jalapeño pepper. Stir in coconut water until well blended. *Makes 2 servings*

Tropical Fruit Fling

Cranberries

Cranberry Apple Twist

   2 apples
   ¾ cup cranberries
   ½ cucumber
   ½ lemon, peeled
   1 inch fresh ginger, peeled

Juice apples, cranberries, cucumber, lemon and ginger. Stir.

Makes 3 servings

Ruby Jewel

   2 cups strawberries
   1½ cups cranberries
   1 orange, peeled

Juice strawberries, cranberries and orange. Stir.   *Makes 2 servings*

Cranberry Apple Twist

Cucumbers

Refreshing Strawberry Juice

2 cups strawberries
1 cucumber
¼ lemon, peeled

Juice strawberries, cucumber and lemon. Stir.   *Makes 2 servings*

Bite-You-Back Veggie Juice

1 cucumber
3 carrots
1 apple
2 stalks celery
3 leaves mustard greens

Juice cucumber, carrots, apple, celery and mustard greens. Stir.

Makes 2 servings

Refreshing Strawberry Juice

Cucumbers

Amazing Green Juice

1 cucumber
1 green apple
2 stalks celery
½ bulb fennel
3 leaves kale

Juice cucumber, apple, celery, fennel and kale. Stir.   *Makes 2 servings*

Cool Cucumber

1 cucumber
¼ pineapple, peeled
¼ cup fresh cilantro

Juice cucumber, pineapple and cilantro. Stir.   *Makes 2 servings*

Cucumbers

Triple Green

½ **honeydew melon, rind removed**
1 **cucumber**
4 **leaves kale**

Juice honeydew, cucumber and kale. Stir.   *Makes 2 servings*

Cucumber Apple Zinger

2 **apples**
½ **cucumber**
1 **inch fresh ginger, peeled**

Juice apples, cucumber and ginger. Stir.   *Makes 2 servings*

Currants

Black Currant Cocktail

2 pears
1 pink grapefruit, peeled
¾ cup black currants
Ice cubes

Juice pears, grapefruit and black currants. Stir. Serve over ice.

Makes 2 servings

Currant Event

1½ cups strawberries
1¼ cups red currants
1 orange, peeled
1 teaspoon honey (optional)

Juice strawberries, currants and orange. Stir in honey, if desired, until well blended. *Makes 2 servings*

Fennel

Fennel Cabbage Juice

1 apple
¼ small green cabbage
½ bulb fennel
1 lemon, peeled

Juice apple, cabbage, fennel and lemon. Stir.   *Makes 2 servings*

Pear-Fennel Juice

2 pears
2 bulbs fennel

Juice pears and fennel. Stir.   *Makes 2 servings*

Fennel Cabbage Juice

Garlic

Cold and Flu Ninja Juice

1 orange, peeled
½ lemon, peeled
⅛ small red onion
1 clove garlic
½ teaspoon honey

Juice orange, lemon, onion and garlic. Stir in honey until well blended.

Makes 1 serving

Heart Healthy Juice

2 tomatoes
1 cup broccoli florets
1 cucumber
1 stalk celery
1 carrot
½ lemon, peeled
1 clove garlic

Juice tomatoes, broccoli, cucumber, celery, carrot, lemon and garlic. Stir.

Makes 2 servings

Cold and Flu Ninja Juice

Ginger

Tangy Twist

1 grapefruit, peeled
4 carrots
1 apple
1 beet
1 inch fresh ginger, peeled
 Ice cubes

Juice grapefruit, carrots, apple, beet and ginger. Stir. Serve over ice.

Makes 3 servings

Up & At 'Em

2 cups fresh spinach
1 apple
1 carrot
1 stalk celery
¼ lemon, peeled
 1 inch fresh ginger, peeled

Juice spinach, apple, carrot, celery, lemon and ginger. Stir.

Makes 2 servings

Ginger

Morning Blend

¼ pineapple, peeled
1 orange, peeled
1 inch fresh ginger, peeled

Juice pineapple, orange and ginger. Stir.   *Makes 2 servings*

Pear Ginger Cocktail

1 pear
½ cucumber
½ lemon, peeled
1 inch fresh ginger, peeled
Ice cubes

Juice pear, cucumber, lemon and ginger. Stir. Serve over ice.

Makes 1 serving

Grapefruit

Immunity Booster

1 grapefruit, peeled
2 oranges, peeled
½ cup blackberries

Juice grapefruit, oranges and blackberries. Stir.   *Makes 3 servings*

Grapefruit Refresher

1 grapefruit, peeled
1 apple
½ cucumber
¼ beet
2 leaves Swiss chard

Juice grapefruit, apple, cucumber, beet and chard. Stir.

Makes 2 servings

Immunity Booster

Grapefruit

Spicy-Sweet Grapefruit

2 grapefruits, peeled
5 carrots
1 inch fresh ginger, peeled

Juice grapefruits, carrots and ginger. Stir.   *Makes 3 servings*

Citrus Blush

1 grapefruit, peeled
1 peach
1 apple

Juice grapefruit, peach and apple. Stir.   *Makes 2 servings*

Spicy-Sweet Grapefruit

Grapes

Purpleberry Juice

2 cups red seedless grapes
1 apple
½ cup blackberries
½ inch fresh ginger, peeled

Juice grapes, apple, blackberries and ginger. Stir.   *Makes 2 servings*

Tart Apple Grape

3 green apples
1 cup green seedless grapes
¼ lemon, peeled

Juice apples, grapes and lemon. Stir.   *Makes 2 servings*

Purpleberry Juice

Green Beans

The Energizer

2 tomatoes
½ cucumber
8 green beans
½ lemon, peeled
Dash hot pepper sauce

Juice tomatoes, cucumber, green beans and lemon. Stir in hot pepper sauce until well blended.   *Makes 2 servings*

Carrot & Green Bean

2 carrots
1 cup green beans

Juice carrots and green beans. Stir.   *Makes 1 serving*

The Energizer

Greens

Waldorf Juice

2 apples
6 leaves beet greens, Swiss chard or kale
2 stalks celery

Juice apples, beet greens and celery. Stir.   *Makes 2 servings*

Calcium-Rich Juice

3 carrots
8 leaves collard greens
1 apple
1 red bell pepper
1 cup fresh cilantro

Juice carrots, collard greens, apple, bell pepper and cilantro. Stir.

Makes 2 servings

Waldorf Juice

Honey

Super C

2 oranges, peeled
1 grapefruit, peeled
1 lemon, peeled
½ cup cranberries
2 teaspoons honey

Juice oranges, grapefruit, lemon and cranberries. Stir in honey until blended.

Makes 3 servings

Honey Spice

1 grapefruit, peeled
¼ pineapple, peeled
½ inch fresh ginger, peeled
4 whole cloves
1 teaspoon honey

Juice grapefruit, pineapple and ginger. Stir. Pour into medium saucepan. Add cloves and honey; simmer over low heat until heated through. Remove from heat; let stand 5 minutes. Strain.

Makes 2 servings

Super C

Honeydew

Melon Raspberry Medley

⅛ **honeydew melon, rind removed**
⅛ **seedless watermelon, rind removed**
⅓ **cup raspberries**
  Ice cubes

Juice honeydew, watermelon and raspberries. Stir. Serve over ice.

Makes 2 servings

Apple Melon Juice

¼ **honeydew melon, rind removed**
¼ **cantaloupe, rind removed**
 1 **apple**
 3 **leaves kale**
 3 **leaves Swiss chard**

Juice honeydew, cantaloupe, apple, kale and chard. Stir.

Makes 2 servings

Melon Raspberry Medley

Jicama

Jicama Pear Carrot

1 cup cut-up peeled jicama

½ pear

2 carrots

½ inch fresh ginger, peeled

Pinch ground red pepper (optional)

Juice jicama, pear, carrots and ginger. Stir in red pepper, if desired, until well blended.   *Makes 1 serving*

Jicama Fruit Combo

1½ cups strawberries

1 cup cut-up peeled jicama

1 apple

½ cucumber

2 sprigs fresh mint

Juice strawberries, jicama, apple, cucumber and mint. Stir.

Makes 2 servings

Jicama Pear Carrot

Kale

Tropical Veggie Juice

   5 leaves kale
   ⅛ pineapple, peeled
   ½ cucumber
   ½ cup coconut water

Juice kale, pineapple and cucumber. Stir in coconut water until well blended. *Makes 2 servings*

Kale Melon

   4 leaves kale
   2 apples
   ⅛ seedless watermelon, rind removed
   ¼ lemon, peeled

Juice kale, apples, watermelon and lemon. Stir. *Makes 2 servings*

Tropical Veggie Juice

Kale

Kale-Apple-Carrot

3 carrots
2 stalks celery
1 apple
3 leaves kale
½ cup fresh parsley

Juice carrots, celery, apple, kale and parsley. Stir.   *Makes 2 servings*

Pears & Greens

3 pears
2 cups fresh spinach
5 leaves kale
1 cucumber
1 cup sugar snap peas
½ lemon, peeled

Juice pears, spinach, kale, cucumber, sugar snap peas and lemon. Stir.

Makes 3 servings

Kiwi

Sweet Green Machine

¼ **honeydew melon, rind removed**
2 **kiwi, peeled**
½ **cup green seedless grapes**

Juice honeydew, kiwi and grapes. Stir.   *Makes 2 servings*

Kiwi Apple Pear

3 **kiwi, peeled**
2 **apples**
1 **pear**

Juice kiwi, apples and pear. Stir.   *Makes 2 servings*

Kiwi

Kiwi Twist

2 kiwi, peeled
2 pears
½ lemon, peeled

Juice kiwi, pears and lemon. Stir.

Makes 2 servings

Apple-K Juice

1 kiwi, peeled
1 apple
3 leaves kale
1 stalk celery
½ lemon, peeled

Juice kiwi, apple, kale, celery and lemon. Stir.

Makes 2 servings

Kiwi Twist

Lemons

Sweet & Spicy Citrus

  5 carrots
  1 orange or 2 clementines, peeled
⅓ cup strawberries
  1 lemon, peeled
½ inch fresh ginger, peeled

Juice carrots, orange, strawberries, lemon and ginger. Stir.

Makes 2 servings

Zesty Vegetable Blend

4 carrots
1 cup broccoli rabe or other dark greens
1 cup watercress
1 (2-inch) piece jicama, peeled
1 lemon, peeled

Juice carrots, broccoli rabe, watercress, jicama and lemon. Stir.

Makes 2 servings

Lemons

Melonade

¼ seedless watermelon, rind removed
1 apple
1 lemon, peeled

Juice watermelon, apple and lemon. Stir.

Makes 4 servings

Pineapple Fizz

½ pineapple, peeled
1 lemon, peeled
Ice cubes
Sparkling water

Juice pineapple and lemon. Stir. Serve over ice; top with sparkling water.

Makes 2 servings

Melonade

Limes

Pomegranate-Lime-Coconut Juice

1 pomegranate, peeled
½ cucumber
1 lime, peeled
¼ cup coconut water

Juice pomegranate seeds, cucumber and lime. Stir in coconut water until well blended. *Makes 2 servings*

Workout Warmup

2 apples
2 kiwi, peeled
½ cup strawberries
4 leaves kale
½ lime, peeled

Juice apples, kiwi, strawberries, kale and lime. Stir. *Makes 2 servings*

Pomegranate-Lime-Coconut Juice

Limes

Mango Tango

1 mango, peeled
1 lime, peeled
½ lemon, peeled
Ice cubes

Juice mango, lime and lemon. Stir. Serve over ice.   *Makes 2 servings*

Grape Lime Juice

1½ cups green seedless grapes
2 limes, peeled

Juice grapes and limes. Stir.   *Makes 1 serving*

Mango Tango

Mangoes

Pineapple-Mango-Cucumber

¼ **pineapple, peeled**
1 **mango, peeled**
1 **cucumber**
½ **lemon, peeled**

Juice pineapple, mango, cucumber and lemon. Stir.

Makes 3 servings

Orange Triple Threat

8 **carrots**
1 **mango, peeled**
1 **orange, peeled**

Juice carrots, mango and orange. Stir.

Makes 3 servings

Pineapple-Mango-Cucumber

Mangoes

Mango-Kiwi-Carrot

1 mango, peeled
2 kiwi, peeled
1 carrot

Juice mango, kiwi and carrot. Stir.   *Makes 2 servings*

Cool Apple Mango

1 mango, peeled
1 apple
1 cucumber
½ inch fresh ginger, peeled

Juice mango, apple, cucumber and ginger. Stir.   *Makes 2 servings*

Mint

Mint Julep Juice

1 apple
1 cup fresh spinach
1 stalk celery
1 cup fresh mint

Juice apple, spinach, celery and mint. Stir.   *Makes 1 serving*

Peach Surprise

1½ cups fresh spinach
1 peach
3 sprigs fresh mint

Juice spinach, peach and mint. Stir.   *Makes 1 serving*

Mint

Mojo Mojito Juice

1 cucumber
1 pear
1 cup fresh mint
½ lime, peeled

Juice cucumber, pear, mint and lime. Stir.   *Makes 2 servings*

Wheatgrass Blast

1 apple
1 cup wheatgrass
½ lemon, peeled
3 springs fresh mint

Juice apple, wheatgrass, lemon and mint. Stir.   *Makes 1 serving*

Onions

Veggie Delight

1 carrot
1 stalk celery
1 beet
1 apple
¼ small sweet onion

Juice carrot, celery, beet, apple and onion. Stir. *Makes 2 servings*

Liquid Salad

2 tomatoes
1 cucumber
½ red bell pepper
1 lemon, peeled
1 cup fresh parsley
1 green onion

Juice tomatoes, cucumber, bell pepper, lemon, parsley and green onion. Stir. *Makes 3 servings*

Oranges

Island Orange Juice

2 oranges, peeled
2 guavas
½ cup strawberries

Juice oranges, guavas and strawberries. Stir.   *Makes 2 servings*

Watermelon Orange

¼ seedless watermelon, rind removed
2 oranges, peeled
   Ice cubes

Juice watermelon and oranges. Stir. Serve over ice.   *Makes 3 servings*

Island Orange Juice

Oranges

Citrus Carrot Juice

1 orange, peeled
2 carrots
½ lemon, peeled

Juice orange, carrots and lemon. Stir.   *Makes 2 servings*

Orange Beet

2 oranges, peeled
1 beet

Juice oranges and beet. Stir.   *Makes 2 servings*

Citrus Carrot Juice

Papaya

Sweet & Sour

1 ½ **cups raspberries**
⅛ **papaya**
½ **grapefruit, peeled**

Juice raspberries, papaya and grapefruit. Stir.   *Makes 2 servings*

Papaya Power Juice

¼ **papaya**
1 **orange, peeled**
¾ **cup fresh parsley**
1 **clove garlic**

Juice papaya, orange, parsley and garlic. Stir.   *Makes 2 servings*

Parsley

Joint Comfort Juice

2 cups fresh spinach

¼ pineapple, peeled

1 pear

1 cup fresh parsley

½ grapefruit, peeled

Juice spinach, pineapple, pear, parsley and grapefruit. Stir.

Makes 2 servings

Rooty Tooty

2 carrots

4 radishes

1 cup fresh parsley

½ cup cut-up peeled rutabaga

Juice carrots, radishes, parsley and rutabaga. Stir. *Makes 2 servings*

138

Joint Comfort Juice

Parsnips

Parsnip-Carrot-Cuke

2 parsnips
2 carrots
½ cucumber
1 lemon, peeled

Juice parsnips, carrots, cucumber and lemon. Stir.   *Makes 2 servings*

Parsnip Party

3 parsnips
1 apple
1 pear
½ bulb fennel
½ cup fresh parsley

Juice parsnips, apple, pear, fennel and parsley. Stir.   *Makes 2 servings*

Parsnip-Carrot-Cuke

Peaches

Peachy Keen

2 peaches
1 cup red seedless grapes
¼ lemon, peeled

Juice peaches, grapes and lemon. Stir.   *Makes 2 servings*

Spiced Peach Pie

1 peach
3 carrots
¼ teaspoon ground cinnamon

Juice peach and carrots. Stir in cinnamon until well blended.

Makes 1 serving

Peachy Keen

Pears

Cool Pear Melon

¼ **honeydew melon, rind removed**

1 **pear**

½ **cucumber**

Juice honeydew, pear and cucumber. Stir.   *Makes 3 servings*

Yellowbelly

¼ **cantaloupe, rind removed**

1 **pear**

2 **parsnips**

¾ **cup cut-up peeled celery root**

½ **inch fresh ginger, peeled**

Juice cantaloupe, pear, parsnips, celery root and ginger. Stir.

Makes 2 servings

Cool Pear Melon

Pears

Cranberry Pear Blast

2 pears
½ cucumber
¾ cup cranberries
¼ lemon, peeled
½ inch fresh ginger, peeled

Juice pears, cucumber, cranberries, lemon and ginger. Stir.

Makes 2 servings

Pear-Carrot-Apple Juice

2 pears
2 carrots
1 apple

Juice pears, carrots and apple. Stir.

Makes 2 servings

Cranberry Pear Blast

Pineapple

Tropical Twist

⅛ **pineapple, peeled**
⅛ **seedless watermelon, rind removed**
1 **orange, peeled**
½ **mango, peeled**
⅓ **cup strawberries**

Juice pineapple, watermelon, orange, mango and strawberries. Stir.

Makes 2 servings

Zippy Apple Pineapple

¼ **pineapple, peeled**
1 **apple**
½ **inch fresh ginger, peeled**

Juice pineapple, apple and ginger. Stir.

Makes 1 serving

Tropical Twist

Pineapple

Spicy Pineapple Carrot

½ **pineapple, peeled**
2 **carrots**
1 **inch fresh ginger, peeled**
  Ice cubes

Juice pineapple, carrots and ginger. Stir. Serve over ice.

Makes 2 servings

Sweet Green Pineapple

¼ **pineapple, peeled**
1 **cup broccoli florets**
1 **carrot**

Juice pineapple, broccoli and carrot. Stir.

Makes 1 serving

Spicy Pineapple Carrot

Plums

Plum Cherry

2 dark plums
1½ cups cherries, pitted

Juice plums and cherries. Stir.   *Makes 2 servings*

Iced Orchard Blend

3 plums
1 apple
  Ice cubes

Juice plums and apple. Stir. Serve over ice.   *Makes 2 servings*

Plum Cherry

Pomegranates

Pomegranate Apple

2 pomegranates, peeled
2 apples

Juice pomegranate seeds and apples. Stir.   *Makes 2 servings*

Pomegranate Kumquat Juice

1 pomegranate, peeled
2 carrots
2 kumquats

Juice pomegranate seeds, carrots and kumquats. Stir.

Makes 1 serving

Pomegranate Apple

Radishes

Hang Loose

5 carrots
2 radishes
½ inch fresh ginger, peeled

Juice carrots, radishes and ginger. Stir. *Makes 1 serving*

Zippy Pineapple Celery

½ pineapple, peeled
2 radishes
1 stalk celery

Juice pineapple, radishes and celery. Stir. *Makes 2 servings*

Radishes

Hot Potato

1 potato
2 carrots
½ cucumber
2 radishes

Juice potato, carrots, cucumber and radishes. Stir.   *Makes 2 servings*

Radical Radish

4 radishes
3 leaves kale
½ cucumber
½ inch fresh ginger, peeled

Juice radishes, kale, cucumber and ginger. Stir.   *Makes 1 serving*

Raspberries

Watermelon Raspberry

¼ seedless watermelon, rind removed
1 cup raspberries
Ice cubes

Juice watermelon and raspberries. Stir. Serve over ice.

Makes 3 servings

Popeye's Favorite Juice

2 cups fresh spinach
¼ pineapple, peeled
1 cup raspberries

Juice spinach, pineapple and raspberries. Stir.

Makes 1 serving

Raspberries

Red Orange Juice

1 orange, peeled
1 apple
½ cup raspberries
½ cup strawberries

Juice orange, apple, raspberries and strawberries. Stir.

Makes 2 servings

Pear Raspberry

2 pears
1½ cups raspberries
½ cucumber

Juice pears, raspberries and cucumber. Stir.

Makes 2 servings

Red Orange Juice

Spinach

Green Juice

2 cups fresh spinach

2 cucumbers

1 pear

½ lemon, peeled

1 inch fresh ginger, peeled

Juice spinach, cucumbers, pear, lemon and ginger. Stir.

Makes 2 servings

Sweet Veggie Juice

1 cup fresh spinach

1 carrot

½ cucumber

1 plum

½ cup strawberries

¼ cup cherries, pitted

Juice spinach, carrot, cucumber, plum, strawberries and cherries. Stir.

Makes 2 servings

Green Juice

Sprouts

Orange Fennel Sprout

2 oranges, peeled
2 stalks celery
1 bulb fennel
1 cup alfalfa sprouts

Juice oranges, celery, fennel and alfalfa sprouts. Stir.

Makes 2 servings

Sprout-Apple-Carrot

2 apples
1 carrot
1 cup alfalfa sprouts
1 cup bean sprouts
4 sprigs fresh parsley

Juice apples, carrot, alfalfa sprouts, bean sprouts and parsley. Stir.

Makes 2 servings

Sprouts

Cool & Crisp

3 stalks celery
2 apples
1 cup alfalfa sprouts
   Ice cubes

Juice celery, apples and alfalfa sprouts. Stir. Serve over ice.

Makes 2 servings

Nutrient-Packed Pear Juice

1½ pears
   ½ cup alfalfa sprouts
   1 clove garlic

Juice pears, alfalfa sprouts and garlic. Stir.   *Makes 1 serving*

Strawberries

Pineapple Berry Delight

½ **pineapple, peeled**
1 **cup fresh spinach**
½ **cup strawberries**
½ **cucumber**

Juice pineapple, spinach, strawberries and cucumber. Stir.

Makes 2 servings

Strawberry Melon

½ **cantaloupe, rind removed**
1 **cup strawberries**

Juice cantaloupe and strawberries. Stir.   *Makes 2 servings*

Strawberries

Sunset Berry

1 cup strawberries
1 orange, peeled
½ lime, peeled

Juice strawberries, orange and lime. Stir.   *Makes 2 servings*

Appleberry Juice

2 apples
1½ cups strawberries
¼ lemon, peeled

Juice apples, strawberries and lemon. Stir.   *Makes 2 servings*

Sunset Berry

Sweet Potatoes

Apple, Tater & Carrot

4 apples
1 sweet potato
1 carrot

Juice apples, sweet potato and carrot. Stir.   *Makes 4 servings*

Garden Juice

2 carrots
1 yellow bell pepper
1 apple
1 cup broccoli florets
1 beet
½ sweet potato
1 cup fresh parsley

Juice carrots, bell pepper, apple, broccoli, beet, sweet potato and parsley. Stir.   *Makes 2 servings*

Apple, Tater & Carrot

Swiss Chard

Double Green Pineapple

4 leaves Swiss chard
4 leaves kale
¼ pineapple, peeled

Juice chard, kale and pineapple. Stir.   *Makes 1 serving*

Rainbow Juice

8 leaves Swiss chard
1 Asian pear
1 apple
1 beet
1 carrot
¼ green cabbage

Juice chard, pear, apple, beet, carrot and cabbage. Stir.

Makes 2 servings

Tangerines

Tangerine Ginger Sipper

  1 tangerine, peeled
  1 pear
  ¼ lemon, peeled
  ½ inch fresh ginger, peeled

Juice tangerine, pear, lemon and ginger. Stir.   *Makes 2 servings*

Fantastic Five Juice

  1 tangerine, peeled
  ½ peach
  ½ apple
  ½ pear
  ½ cup green seedless grapes

Juice tangerine, peach, apple, pear and grapes. Stir.

Makes 2 servings

Tangerine Ginger Sipper

Tomatoes

Pink Power Juice

¼ seedless watermelon, rind removed

1 tomato

1 lemon, peeled

Juice watermelon, tomato and lemon. Stir.

Makes 2 servings

Gazpacho in a Glass

3 tomatoes

2 cucumbers

3 stalks celery

1 apple

1 lemon, peeled

1 green onion

¼ cup fresh cilantro

1 chile pepper

1 clove garlic

Pinch black pepper

Juice tomatoes, cucumbers, celery, apple, lemon, green onion, cilantro, chile pepper and garlic. Stir in black pepper until blended.

Makes 4 servings

Tomatoes

Garden Fresh

3 tomatoes

3 carrots

2 radishes

Juice tomatoes, carrots and radishes. Stir.

Makes 3 servings

Migraine Blaster

3 carrots

3 apples

1 cup red seedless grapes

1 tomato

1 stalk celery

Juice carrots, apples, grapes, tomato and celery. Stir.

Makes 2 servings

Garden Fresh

Turnips

Back to Your Roots

2 beets
2 carrots
2 parsnips
1 turnip
1 sweet potato

Juice beets, carrots, parsnips, turnip and sweet potato. Stir.

Makes 3 servings

Turnip Blast

2 carrots
1 turnip
1 pear
1 cup fresh parsley
½ lemon, peeled

Juice carrots, turnip, pear, parsley and lemon. Stir.   *Makes 2 servings*

180

Watercress

Easy Being Green

    2 cups watercress
    2 parsnips
    2 stalks celery
    ½ cucumber
    4 sprigs fresh basil

Juice watercress, parsnips, celery, cucumber and basil. Stir.

Makes 2 servings

Beet Still My Heart

    3 carrots
    1 beet
    ½ cup watercress
    ½ small red onion
    1 clove garlic

Juice carrots, beet, watercress, onion and garlic. Stir.

Makes 2 servings

Easy Being Green

Watermelon

Pretty in Pink

¼ **seedless watermelon, rind removed**
1½ **cups cranberries**
½ **cucumber**

Juice watermelon, cranberries and cucumber. Stir.   *Makes 3 servings*

Double Melon Orange

⅛ **seedless watermelon, rind removed**
⅛ **cantaloupe, rind removed**
1 **orange, peeled**

Juice watermelon, cantaloupe and orange. Stir.   *Makes 2 servings*

Pretty in Pink

Zucchini

Invigorating Greens & Citrus

2 oranges, peeled
1 grapefruit, peeled
1 zucchini
½ cup broccoli florets
½ inch fresh ginger, peeled

Juice oranges, grapefruit, zucchini, broccoli and ginger. Stir.

Makes 2 servings

Simple Garden Blend

3 carrots
2 apples
1 zucchini

Juice carrots, apples and zucchini. Stir.   *Makes 2 servings*

A

Apples, 9, 24
Amazing Green Juice, 82
Appleberry Juice, 168
Apple Carrot Zinger, 60
Apple-K Juice, 114
Apple Melon Juice, 106
Apple, Tater & Carrot, 170
Arthritis Tonic, 32
Autumn Apple Pie Juice, 52
Bite-You-Back Veggie Juice, 80
Blueberry Haze, 44
Cabbage Patch Juice, 54
Calcium-Rich Juice, 102
Carotene with a Kick, 62
Celery Root-Beet-Carrot
 Juice, 68
Cherry Green, 70
Citrus Blush, 96
Cool & Crisp, 166
Cool Apple Mango, 126
Cranberry Apple Twist, 78
Crimson Carrot, 56
Cucumber Apple Zinger, 84
Cucumber Basil Cooler, 34
Drinkable Slaw, 48
Drink a Rainbow, 50
Early Riser Breakfast, 36
Fennel Cabbage Juice, 86
Garden Juice, 170
Gazpacho in a Glass, 176
Grapefruit Refresher, 94
Green Berry Booster, 44
Green Energy, 68
Headache Buster, 64
Iced Orchard Blend, 152
Jicama Fruit Combo, 108
Kale & Fruit Juice, 42
Kale-Apple-Carrot, 112
Kale Melon, 110
Kiwi Apple Pear, 113
Mean and Green, 24
Melonade, 118
Migraine Blaster, 178
Mint Julep Juice, 127
Orchard Crush, 26
Parsnip Party, 140
Pear Cabbage Juice, 56
Pear-Carrot-Apple Juice, 146
Pomegranate Apple, 154
Purpleberry Juice, 98
Rainbow Juice, 172

Apples *(continued)*
Really Rhubarb, 24
Red Orange Juice, 160
Ruby Apple Stinger, 38
Sharp Apple Cooler, 28
Simple Garden Blend, 186
Spicy Apple Peach, 26
Sprout-Apple-Carrot, 164
Super Beta-Carotene, 46
Sweet Celery, 66
Tangerapple, 28
Tangy Twist, 90
Tart Apple Grape, 98
Tongue Twister, 76
Triple Pepper, 40
Up & At 'Em, 90
Veggie Blast, 74
Veggie Delight, 130
Waldorf Juice, 102
Wheatgrass Blast, 128
Workout Warmup, 120
Zippy Apple Pineapple, 148
Apricots, 9, 30
Orange Apricot, 30
Star of the Show, 30
Asparagus, 9, 32
Arthritis Tonic, 32
Spring Green Cocktail, 32

B

Basil, 10, 34
Cucumber Basil Cooler, 34
Easy Being Green, 182
Tangy Tomato Basil, 34
Beets, 10, 36
Back to Your Roots, 180
Beet Still My Heart, 182
Celery Root-Beet-Carrot
 Juice, 68
Drink a Rainbow, 50
Early Riser Breakfast, 36
Fiery Cucumber Beet Juice,
 72
Garden Juice, 170
Orange Beet, 134
Purple Pineapple Juice, 36
Rainbow Juice, 172
Ruby Apple Stinger, 38
Tangy Twist, 90
Veggie Blast, 74
Veggie Chiller, 38
Veggie Delight, 130

Blackberries, 10, 42
Immunity Booster, 94
Kale & Fruit Juice, 42
Purpleberry Juice, 98
Super Berry Refresher, 42
Blueberries, 11, 44
Blueberry Haze, 44
Green Berry Booster, 44
Super Berry Refresher, 42
Bok Choy, 11, 46
Cleansing Green Juice, 46
Super Beta-Carotene, 46
Broccoli, 11, 48
Arthritis Tonic, 32
Drinkable Slaw, 48
Drink a Rainbow, 50
Garden Juice, 170
Headache Buster, 64
Healthy Complexion Combo, 60
Heart Healthy Juice, 88
Invigorating Greens & Citrus,
 186
Sweet & Green, 48
Sweet Green Pineapple, 150
Zesty Vegetable Blend, 116
Brussels Sprouts, 11, 50
Citrus Sprout, 50
Drink a Rainbow, 50
Butternut Squash, 12, 52
Autumn Apple Pie Juice, 52
Butternut Sparkler, 52

C

Cabbage, 12, 54
Cabbage Patch Juice, 54
Crimson Carrot, 56
Drinkable Slaw, 48
Early Riser Breakfast, 36
Fennel Cabbage Juice, 86
Pear Cabbage Juice, 56
Rabbit Juice, 40
Rainbow Juice, 172
Red Cabbage & Pineapple,
 54
Cantaloupe, 12, 57
Apple Melon Juice, 106
Cantaloupe & Grape, 58
Cantaloupe Ginger, 57
Cherry & Melon, 70
Double Melon Orange, 184
Melon Refresher, 58
Strawberry Melon, 167

Index

Cantaloupe *(continued)*
Vitamin Blast, 57
Yellowbelly, 144
Carrots, 12, 60
Apple Carrot Zinger, 60
Apple, Tater & Carrot, 170
Arthritis Tonic, 32
Back to Your Roots, 180
Beet Still My Heart, 182
Bite-You-Back Veggie Juice, 80
Butternut Sparkler, 52
Calcium-Rich Juice, 102
Carotene with a Kick, 62
Carrot & Green Bean, 100
Celery Root-Beet-Carrot Juice, 68
Citrus Carrot Juice, 134
Crimson Carrot, 56
Drinkable Slaw, 48
Drink a Rainbow, 50
Early Riser Breakfast, 36
Garden Fresh, 178
Garden Juice, 170
Hang Loose, 156
Healthy Complexion Combo, 60
Heart Healthy Juice, 88
Hot Potato, 158
Hotsy Totsy, 72
Jicama Pear Carrot, 108
Kale & Fruit Juice, 42
Kale-Apple-Carrot, 112
Mango-Kiwi-Carrot, 126
Migraine Blaster, 178
Orange Triple Threat, 124
Parsnip-Carrot-Cuke, 140
Pear Cabbage Juice, 56
Pear-Carrot-Apple Juice, 146
Pomegranate Kumquat Juice, 154
Rainbow Juice, 172
Rooty Tooty, 138
Ruby Apple Stinger, 38
Simple Garden Blend, 186
Spiced Peach Pie, 142
Spicy Pineapple Carrot, 150
Spicy-Sweet Grapefruit, 96
Sprout-Apple-Carrot, 164
Super Beta-Carotene, 46
Sweet & Spicy Citrus, 116
Sweet Green Pineapple, 150

Carrots *(continued)*
Sweet Pepper Carrot, 62
Sweet Veggie Juice, 162
Tangy Twist, 90
Turnip Blast, 180
Up & At 'Em, 90
Veggie Blast, 74
Veggie Chiller, 38
Veggie Delight, 130
Zesty Vegetable Blend, 116
Cauliflower, 13, 64
Drink a Rainbow, 50
Headache Buster, 64
Tomato with a Twist, 64
Celery, 13, 66
Amazing Green Juice, 82
Apple-K Juice, 114
Arthritis Tonic, 32
Bedtime Cocktail, 66
Bite-You-Back Veggie Juice, 80
Celery Root-Beet-Carrot Juice, 68
Cherry Green, 70
Cleansing Green Juice, 46
Cool & Crisp, 166
Easy Being Green, 182
Gazpacho in a Glass, 176
Green Energy, 68
Green Queen, 74
Heart Healthy Juice, 88
Kale-Apple-Carrot, 112
Mean and Green, 24
Migraine Blaster, 178
Mint Julep Juice, 127
Orange Fennel Sprout, 164
Spicy Apple Peach, 26
Sweet & Green, 48
Sweet Celery, 66
Up & At 'Em, 90
Veggie Blast, 74
Veggie Delight, 130
Waldorf Juice, 102
Yellowbelly, 144
Zippy Pineapple Celery, 156
Cherries, 13, 70
Cherry & Melon, 70
Cherry Green, 70
Plum Cherry, 152
Sweet Veggie Juice, 162

Cilantro, 14, 74
Calcium-Rich Juice, 102
Cool Cucumber, 82
Gazpacho in a Glass, 176
Green Queen, 74
Hotsy Totsy, 72
Tongue Twister, 76
Veggie Blast, 74
Coconut Water, 14, 76
Pomegranate-Lime-Coconut Juice, 120
Tongue Twister, 76
Tropical Fruit Fling, 76
Tropical Veggie Juice, 110
Cranberries, 14, 78
Cranberry Apple Twist, 78
Cranberry Pear Blast, 146
Pretty in Pink, 184
Ruby Jewel, 78
Super C, 104
Cucumbers, 14, 80
Amazing Green Juice, 82
Bite-You-Back Veggie Juice, 80
Cool Apple Mango, 126
Cool Cucumber, 82
Cucumber Apple Zinger, 84
Cucumber Basil Cooler, 34
Fiery Cucumber Beet Juice, 72
Gazpacho in a Glass, 176
Green Berry Booster, 44
Green Juice, 162
Healthy Complexion Combo, 60
Heart Healthy Juice, 88
Liquid Salad, 130
Mean and Green, 24
Mojo Mojito Juice, 128
Parsnip-Carrot-Cuke, 140
Pears & Greens, 112
Pineapple-Mango-Cucumber, 124
Refreshing Strawberry Juice, 80
Sharp Apple Cooler, 28
Spring Green Cocktail, 32
Super Berry Refresher, 42
Triple Green, 84

Index

Currants, 14, 85
 Black Currant Cocktail, 85
 Currant Event, 85

F

Fennel, 15, 86
 Fennel Cabbage Juice, 86
 Orange Fennel Sprout, 164
 Parsnip Party, 140
 Pear-Fennel Juice, 86

G

Garlic, 15, 88
 Beet Still My Heart, 182
 Cold and Flu Ninja Juice, 88
 Gazpacho in a Glass, 176
 Heart Healthy Juice, 88
 Nutrient-Packed Pear Juice,
  166
 Papaya Power Juice, 136

Ginger, 15, 90
 Apple Carrot Zinger, 60
 Blueberry Haze, 44
 Cantaloupe Ginger, 57
 Celery Root-Beet-Carrot
  Juice, 68
 Cool Apple Mango, 126
 Cranberry Apple Twist, 78
 Cranberry Pear Blast, 146
 Cucumber Apple Zinger, 84
 Drinkable Slaw, 48
 Fiery Cucumber Beet Juice,
  72
 Green Energy, 68
 Green Juice, 162
 Green Queen, 74
 Hang Loose, 156
 Honey Spice, 104
 Invigorating Greens & Citrus,
  186
 Jicama Pear Carrot, 108
 Mean and Green, 24
 Morning Blend, 92
 Pear Cabbage Juice, 56
 Pear Ginger Cocktail, 92
 Purpleberry Juice, 98
 Purple Pineapple Juice, 36
 Radical Radish, 158
 Ruby Apple Stinger, 38
 Sharp Apple Cooler, 28
 Spicy Pineapple Carrot, 150
 Spicy-Sweet Grapefruit, 96
 Super Beta-Carotene, 46

Ginger *(continued)*
 Sweet & Spicy Citrus, 116
 Tangerine Ginger Sipper,
  174
 Tangy Twist, 90
 Up & At 'Em, 90
 Veggie Blast, 74
 Yellowbelly, 144
 Zippy Apple Pineapple, 148

Grapefruit, 15, 94
 Black Currant Cocktail, 85
 Blueberry Haze, 44
 Citrus Blush, 96
 Grapefruit Refresher, 94
 Honey Spice, 104
 Immunity Booster, 94
 Invigorating Greens & Citrus,
  186
 Joint Comfort Juice, 138
 Spicy-Sweet Grapefruit, 96
 Super C, 104
 Sweet & Sour, 136
 Tangy Twist, 90

Grapes, 16, 98
 Cantaloupe & Grape, 58
 Crimson Carrot, 56
 Grape Lime Juice, 122
 Migraine Blaster, 178
 Peachy Keen, 142
 Purpleberry Juice, 98
 Sweet Green Machine, 113
 Tangerine Ginger Sipper,
  174
 Tart Apple Grape, 98

Green Beans, 16, 100
 Carrot & Green Bean,
  100
 The Energizer, 100

Greens, 16, 102
 Bite-You-Back Veggie Juice,
  80
 Calcium-Rich Juice, 102
 Green Berry Booster, 44
 Spicy Apple Peach, 26
 Waldorf Juice, 102

H

Honey, 16, 104
 Cold and Flu Ninja Juice,
  88
 Honey Spice, 104
 Super C, 104

Honeydew, 16, 106
 Apple Melon Juice, 106
 Cool Pear Melon, 144
 Melon Raspberry Medley,
  106
 Sweet Green Machine, 113
 Triple Green, 84

J

Jicama, 17, 108
 Jicama Fruit Combo, 108
 Jicama Pear Carrot, 108
 Zesty Vegetable Blend, 116

K

Kale, 17, 110
 Amazing Green Juice, 82
 Apple-K Juice, 114
 Apple Melon Juice, 106
 Double Green Pineapple, 172
 Green Energy, 68
 Green Queen, 74
 Kale & Fruit Juice, 42
 Kale-Apple-Carrot, 112
 Kale Melon, 110
 Mean and Green, 24
 Pears & Greens, 112
 Radical Radish, 158
 Super Beta-Carotene, 46
 Triple Green, 84
 Tropical Veggie Juice, 110
 Veggie Blast, 74
 Workout Warmup, 120

Kiwi, 17, 113
 Apple-K Juice, 114
 Kiwi Apple Pear, 113
 Kiwi Twist, 114
 Mango-Kiwi-Carrot, 126
 Spicy Apple Peach, 26
 Sweet Green Machine, 113
 Workout Warmup, 120

L

Lemons, 17, 116
 Cherry Green, 70
 Fennel Cabbage Juice, 86
 Fiery Cucumber Beet Juice, 72
 Gazpacho in a Glass, 176
 Liquid Salad, 130
 Melonade, 118
 Parsnip-Carrot-Cuke, 140
 Pineapple Fizz, 118
 Pink Power Juice, 176

189

Index

Lemons *(continued)*
Super C, 104
Sweet & Spicy Citrus, 116
Sweet Celery, 66
Zesty Vegetable Blend, 116
Limes, 17, 120
Grape Lime Juice, 122
Mango Tango, 122
Melon Refresher, 58
Pomegranate-Lime-Coconut
Juice, 120
Workout Warmup, 120

M
Mangoes, 18, 124
Cool Apple Mango, 126
Mango-Kiwi-Carrot, 126
Mango Tango, 122
Orange Triple Threat, 124
Pineapple-Mango-Cucumber,
124
Tropical Fruit Fling, 76
Tropical Twist, 148
Mint, 18, 127
Jicama Fruit Combo, 108
Melon Refresher, 58
Mint Julep Juice, 127
Mojo Mojito Juice, 128
Peach Surprise, 127
Sharp Apple Cooler, 28
Wheatgrass Blast, 128

O
Onions, 18, 130
Beet Still My Heart, 182
Cold and Flu Ninja Juice,
88
Gazpacho in a Glass, 176
Liquid Salad, 130
Veggie Delight, 130
Oranges, 18, 132
Citrus Carrot Juice, 134
Citrus Sprout, 50
Cold and Flu Ninja Juice,
88
Currant Event, 85
Double Melon Orange, 184
Early Riser Breakfast, 36
Immunity Booster, 94
Invigorating Greens & Cltrus,
186
Island Orange Juice, 132
Kale & Fruit Juice, 42

Oranges *(continued)*
Morning Blend, 92
Orange Apricot, 30
Orange Beet, 134
Orange Fennel Sprout, 164
Orange Triple Threat, 124
Papaya Power Juice, 136
Red Orange Juice, 160
Ruby Jewel, 78
Sunset Berry, 168
Super C, 104
Sweet & Spicy Citrus, 116
Tropical Fruit Fling, 76
Tropical Twist, 148
Vitamin Blast, 57
Watermelon Orange, 132

P
Papaya, 19, 136
Papaya Power Juice, 136
Sweet & Sour, 136
Vitamin Blast, 57
Parsley, 19, 138
Arthritis Tonic, 32
Cherry Green, 70
Garden Juice, 170
Joint Comfort Juice, 138
Kale-Apple-Carrot, 112
Liquid Salad, 130
Papaya Power Juice, 136
Parsnip Party, 140
Rabbit Juice, 40
Rooty Tooty, 138
Sprout-Apple-Carrot, 164
Turnip Blast, 180
Parsnips, 19, 140
Back to Your Roots, 180
Easy Being Green, 182
Parsnip-Carrot-Cuke, 140
Parsnip Party, 140
Yellowbelly, 144
Peaches, 19, 142
Citrus Blush, 96
Peach Surprise, 127
Peachy Keen, 142
Spiced Peach Pie, 142
Spicy Apple Peach, 26
Star of the Show, 30
Pears, 20, 144
Black Currant Cocktail, 85
Cool Pear Melon, 144
Cranberry Pear Blast, 146

Pears *(continued)*
Drink a Rainbow, 50
Green Juice, 162
Jicama Pear Carrot, 108
Joint Comfort Juice, 138
Kiwi Apple Pear, 113
Kiwi Twist, 114
Melon Refresher, 58
Mojo Mojito Juice, 128
Nutrient-Packed Pear Juice,
166
Parsnip Party, 140
Pear Cabbage Juice, 56
Pear-Carrot-Apple-Juice,
146
Pear-Fennel Juice, 86
Pear Ginger Cocktail, 92
Pear Raspberry, 160
Pears & Greens, 112
Purple Pineapple Juice, 36
Rainbow Juice, 172
Pear Raspberry, 160
Tangerine Ginger Sipper,
174
Turnip Blast, 180
Yellowbelly, 144
Peppers, Bell, 10, 40
Calcium-Rich Juice, 102
Garden Juice, 170
Rabbit Juice, 40
Sweet Pepper Carrot, 62
Triple Pepper, 40
Veggie Blast, 74
Peppers, Chile, 13, 72
Fiery Cucumber Beet Juice,
72
Gazpacho in a Glass, 176
Hotsy Totsy, 72
Tongue Twister, 76
Triple Pepper, 40
Pineapple, 20, 148
Cool Cucumber, 82
Double Green Pineapple, 172
Drink a Rainbow, 50
Honey Spice, 104
Hotsy Totsy, 72
Joint Comfort Juice, 138
Morning Blend, 92
Pineapple Berry Delight, 167
Pineapple Fizz, 118
Pineapple-Mango-Cucumber,
124

Pineapple *(continued)*
Popeye's Favorite Juice, 159
Purple Pineapple Juice, 36
Red Cabbage & Pineapple, 54
Spicy Pineapple Carrot, 150
Star of the Show, 30
Sweet & Green, 48
Sweet Green Pineapple, 150
Tropical Fruit Fling, 76
Tropical Twist, 148
Tropical Veggie Juice, 110
Zippy Apple Pineapple, 148
Zippy Pineapple Celery, 156
Plums, 20, 152
Iced Orchard Blend, 152
Plum Cherry, 152
Star of the Show, 30
Sweet Veggie Juice, 162
Pomegranates, 20, 154
Butternut Sparkler, 52
Pomegranate Apple, 154
Pomegranate Kumquat Juice, 154
Pomegranate-Lime-Coconut Juice, 120

R
Radishes, 21, 156
Carotene with a Kick, 62
Garden Fresh, 178
Hang Loose, 156
Hot Potato, 158
Radical Radish, 158
Rooty Tooty, 138
Veggie Blast, 74
Zippy Pineapple Celery, 156
Raspberries, 21, 159
Melon Raspberry Medley, 106
Orchard Crush, 26
Pear Raspberry, 160
Popeye's Favorite Juice, 159
Red Orange Juice, 160
Super Berry Refresher, 42
Sweet & Sour, 136
Sweet Celery, 66
Watermelon Raspberry, 159

S
Spinach, 21, 162
Green Energy, 68
Green Juice, 162
Green Queen, 74

Spinach *(continued)*
Joint Comfort Juice, 138
Mint Julep Juice, 127
Peach Surprise, 127
Pears & Greens, 112
Pineapple Berry Delight, 167
Popeye's Favorite Juice, 159
Sweet Veggie Juice, 162
Tangy Tomato Basil, 34
Up & At 'Em, 90
Sprouts, 21, 164
Cool & Crisp, 166
Nutrient-Packed Pear Juice, 166
Orange Fennel Sprout, 164
Sprout-Apple-Carrot, 164
Strawberries, 22, 167
Appleberry Juice, 168
Currant Event, 85
Island Orange Juice, 132
Jicama Fruit Combo, 108
Orchard Crush, 26
Pineapple Berry Delight, 167
Red Orange Juice, 160
Refreshing Strawberry Juice, 80
Ruby Jewel, 78
Strawberry Melon, 167
Sunset Berry, 168
Super Berry Refresher, 42
Sweet & Spicy Citrus, 116
Sweet Veggie Juice, 162
Tropical Fruit Fling, 76
Tropical Twist, 148
Workout Warmup, 120
Sweet Potatoes, 22, 170
Apple, Tater & Carrot, 170
Back to Your Roots, 180
Garden Juice, 170
Swiss Chard, 22, 172
Apple Melon Juice, 106
Carotene with a Kick, 62
Double Green Pineapple, 172
Grapefruit Refresher, 94
Rainbow Juice, 172
Vitamin Blast, 57

T
Tangerines, 22, 174
Fantastic Five Juice, 174
Tangerapple, 28
Tangerine Ginger Sipper, 174

Tomatoes, 22, 176
Drink a Rainbow, 50
Garden Fresh, 178
Gazpacho in a Glass, 176
Healthy Complexion Combo, 60
Heart Healthy Juice, 88
Liquid Salad, 130
Migraine Blaster, 178
Pink Power Juice, 176
Rabbit Juice, 40
Spring Green Cocktail, 32
Tangy Tomato Basil, 34
The Energizer, 100
Tomato with a Twist, 64
Veggie Blast, 74
Turnips, 23, 180
Back to Your Roots, 180
Turnip Blast, 180

W
Watercress, 23, 182
Beet Still My Heart, 182
Easy Being Green, 182
Healthy Complexion Combo, 60
Zesty Vegetable Blend, 116
Watermelon, 23, 184
Cherry & Melon, 70
Double Melon Orange, 184
Kale Melon, 110
Melonade, 118
Melon Raspberry Medley, 106
Pink Power Juice, 176
Pretty in Pink, 184
Tropical Twist, 148
Watermelon Orange, 132
Watermelon Raspberry, 159

Z
Zucchini, 23, 186
Invigorating Greens & Citrus, 186
Simple Garden Blend, 186

METRIC CONVERSION CHART

VOLUME MEASUREMENTS (dry)

$1/8$ teaspoon = 0.5 mL
$1/4$ teaspoon = 1 mL
$1/2$ teaspoon = 2 mL
$3/4$ teaspoon = 4 mL
1 teaspoon = 5 mL
1 tablespoon = 15 mL
2 tablespoons = 30 mL
$1/4$ cup = 60 mL
$1/3$ cup = 75 mL
$1/2$ cup = 125 mL
$2/3$ cup = 150 mL
$3/4$ cup = 175 mL
1 cup = 250 mL
2 cups = 1 pint = 500 mL
3 cups = 750 mL
4 cups = 1 quart = 1 L

VOLUME MEASUREMENTS (fluid)

1 fluid ounce (2 tablespoons) = 30 mL
4 fluid ounces ($1/2$ cup) = 125 mL
8 fluid ounces (1 cup) = 250 mL
12 fluid ounces ($1 1/2$ cups) = 375 mL
16 fluid ounces (2 cups) = 500 mL

WEIGHTS (mass)

$1/2$ ounce = 15 g
1 ounce = 30 g
3 ounces = 90 g
4 ounces = 120 g
8 ounces = 225 g
10 ounces = 285 g
12 ounces = 360 g
16 ounces = 1 pound = 450 g

DIMENSIONS

$1/16$ inch = 2 mm
$1/8$ inch = 3 mm
$1/4$ inch = 6 mm
$1/2$ inch = 1.5 cm
$3/4$ inch = 2 cm
1 inch = 2.5 cm

OVEN TEMPERATURES

250°F = 120°C
275°F = 140°C
300°F = 150°C
325°F = 160°C
350°F = 180°C
375°F = 190°C
400°F = 200°C
425°F = 220°C
450°F = 230°C

BAKING PAN SIZES

Utensil	Size in Inches/Quarts	Metric Volume	Size in Centimeters
Baking or Cake Pan (square or rectangular)	$8 \times 8 \times 2$	2 L	$20 \times 20 \times 5$
	$9 \times 9 \times 2$	2.5 L	$23 \times 23 \times 5$
	$12 \times 8 \times 2$	3 L	$30 \times 20 \times 5$
	$13 \times 9 \times 2$	3.5 L	$33 \times 23 \times 5$
Loaf Pan	$8 \times 4 \times 3$	1.5 L	$20 \times 10 \times 7$
	$9 \times 5 \times 3$	2 L	$23 \times 13 \times 7$
Round Layer Cake Pan	$8 \times 1 1/2$	1.2 L	20×4
	$9 \times 1 1/2$	1.5 L	23×4
Pie Plate	$8 \times 1 1/4$	750 mL	20×3
	$9 \times 1 1/4$	1 L	23×3
Baking Dish or Casserole	1 quart	1 L	—
	$1 1/2$ quart	1.5 L	—
	2 quart	2 L	—